Karsh: The Art of the Portrait

Karsh: The Art of the Portrait

Essays by James Borcoman
Estelle Jussim
Philip J. Pocock
Lilly Koltun

Produced in collaboration with
the National Archives of Canada

National Gallery of Canada
Ottawa, 1989

The National Gallery of Canada and the National
Archives of Canada acknowledge the generous
assistance of IBM Canada Ltd.

Few have created images as lasting as those made
by Canadian photographer Yousuf Karsh. His
portraits have brought an entire world nearer to
the great personalities of this century. Thus IBM
Canada is delighted, in this, photography's one
hundred and fiftieth anniversary year, to have an
opportunity to sponsor the first major retrospective of Karsh's work. Some of the works will
undoubtedly be familiar; others are being shown
for the first time. But all of them display the genius
of a man who once said "I have always been in
quest of a secret – the mind and soul behind the
human face."

John M. Thompson
Chairman and Chief Executive Officer
IBM Canada Ltd.

Contents

Foreword

Dr. Shirley L. Thomson
Director
National Gallery of Canada

The National Gallery of Canada has a long tradition of supporting photography as an art form. Its series of annual exhibitions, the Canadian International Salon of Photographic Art, held from 1934 to 1939, attracted contributions from leading photographers from around the world, including the young Yousuf Karsh.

In 1960, the National Gallery mounted the first solo exhibition of Yousuf Karsh's work to be held in an art museum. When it opened in Ottawa, Charles Comfort, Director from 1960 to 1965, spoke of Karsh's ability to establish "the indisputable framework of identity, and simultaneously [surround] the separate personalities with a penumbra of artistry, that sets each study apart as an individual discovery ... ."

In 1967 the National Gallery began to collect works. Jean Sutherland Boggs, Director from 1966 to 1976, astutely foresaw the art world's acceptance of photography as a valid artistic medium. Shortly after her arrival she appointed James Borcoman as Curator, Photographs Collection, and gave him the task of establishing an historical and international collection of photographs as works of art. Now, one hundred and fifty years after the birth of photography, the Gallery has achieved world-wide recognition for the importance of its Photographs Collection.

Together, the National Archives of Canada, with its vast collection which documents the history of photography in Canada, the Canadian Museum of Contemporary Photography, an affiliate of the Gallery, which represents contemporary photography in Canada, and the National Gallery, with its collection which emphasizes photography outside Canada, have established an historical and international context for Canadian photography.

It seems fitting therefore that the National Gallery of Canada, in collaboration with the National Archives of Canada, should present a retrospective exhibition of Karsh's work as part of photography's world-wide birthday celebrations – fitting not only because Karsh is Canada's best-known photographer, but also because of the important role portraiture has played in the history of the medium.

There is an even more satisfying reason for holding this exhibition. Yousuf Karsh has made a generous gift of almost one hundred of his best-known photographs to the Gallery. The publication and the exhibition become the occasion to honour the artist both for his generosity and for the splendid contribution his photographs will make to our collection.

Thanks to the National Archives, which has shared in the production costs, and with the assistance of IBM Canada Ltd., this retrospective is the largest exhibition ever to be presented of Karsh's œuvre, and includes many works never before shown or published; and the accompanying monograph is the most detailed examination of his art to appear in print. As a major lender to the exhibition, the National Archives's role has been crucial and we are grateful for its contribution.

Dr. Jean-Pierre Wallot
National Archivist
National Archives of Canada

Among the many pleasures of an archivist's life, there is one which stands out for its excitement and abiding sense of accomplishment. This is the pleasure of acquiring a truly great archival collection for future generations, one which will always challenge researchers, stimulate thought, and stir admiration, both for its substance and for the grace and profundity with which that substance is expressed. Such a collection is the archive of Yousuf Karsh.

The impressive volume of photography generated by Karsh over his wide-ranging career documents an entire stratum of Canadian and international society in the modern age. But his work is not the mere cataloguing of faces and names, irreplaceable though this may be to the historical record. It is not the death of the soul captured by the camera, as some early superstitions about the new technology of photography would have it. It is instead the perpetual enlivening of the soul. Karsh's talent creates a new and enduring life for his sitters, as he brings out their unique characters through his perceptive lens and gives history a human face.

This publication, and the exhibition which engendered it, by presenting some of the breadth and richness of the Karsh archive, underscores the essential role of the archival profession in preserving our collective heritage, our very identity. Beyond the boundaries of any one country, every country shares in a communal need, lofty yet heartfelt, to retain and keep safe those records of ourselves which are the memory of our existence on the planet. Little can symbolize this need more clearly than the Karsh Collection, created by a cosmopolitan "citizen of the world" who is also a well-rooted Canadian. It is a Canadian and an international treasure which Canada is honoured to hold.

Therefore, it is my great pleasure to have the National Archives participate with the National Gallery in this endeavour. Together, as national cultural institutions, we have an opportunity to reveal the scope of the achievements of Canada's best known and most beloved portrait photographer. Moreover, we have an ideal occasion to celebrate jointly both Karsh's eightieth birthday and the commemoration of one hundred and fifty years since the invention of his medium: photography.

9

15

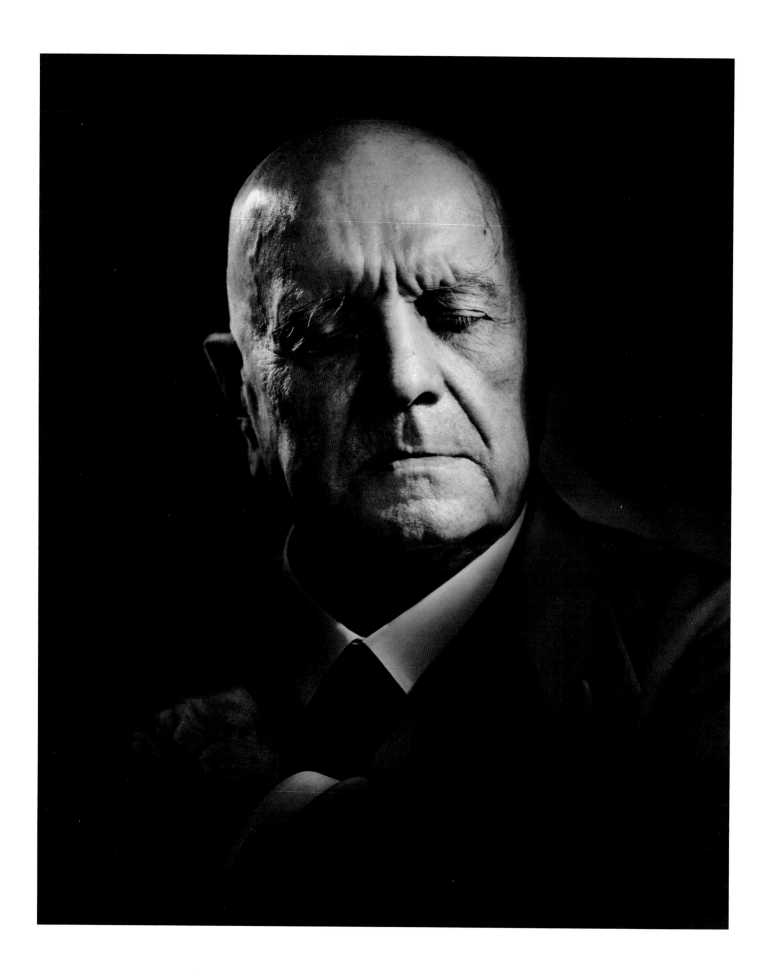

21

25

33

39

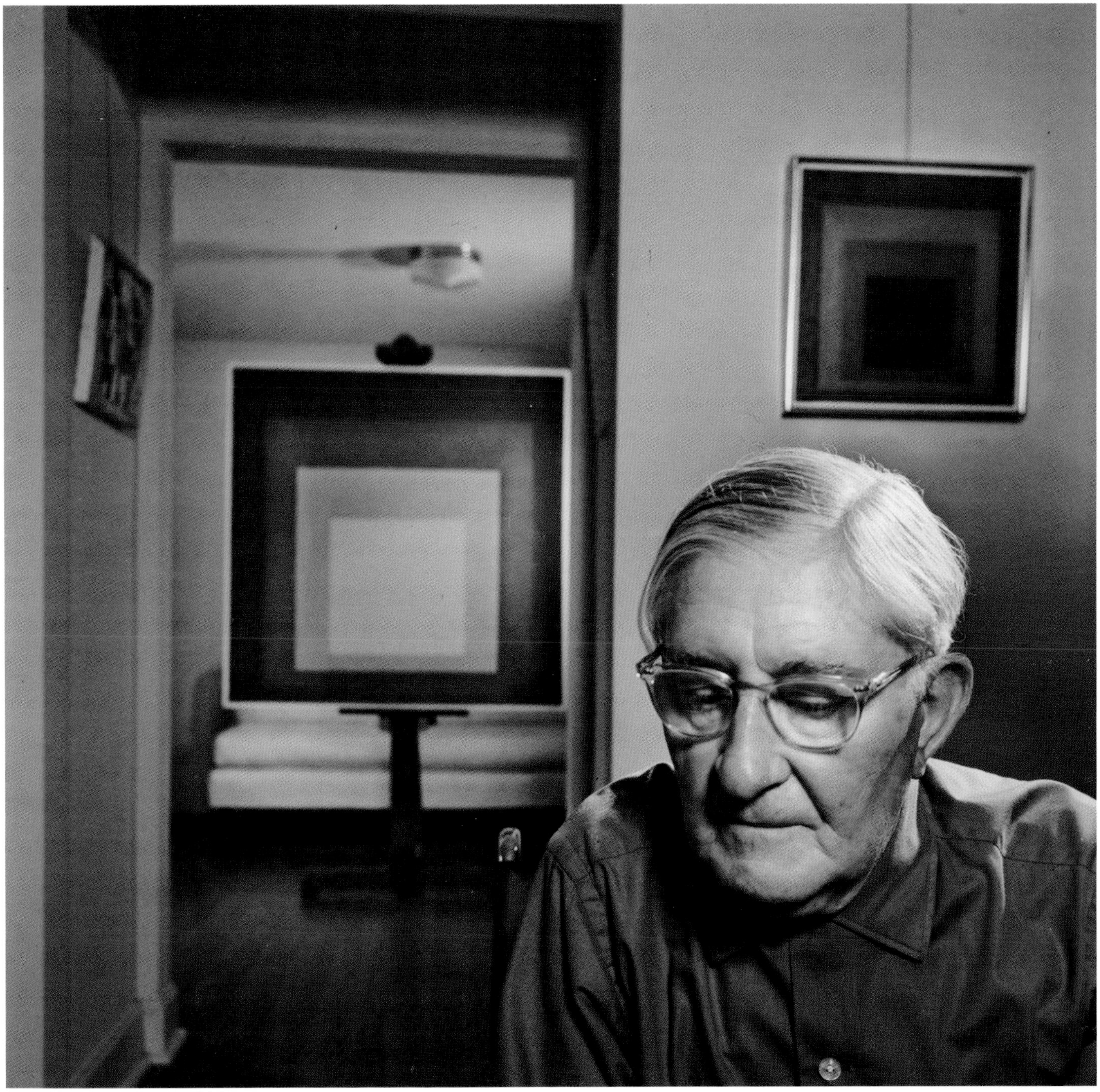

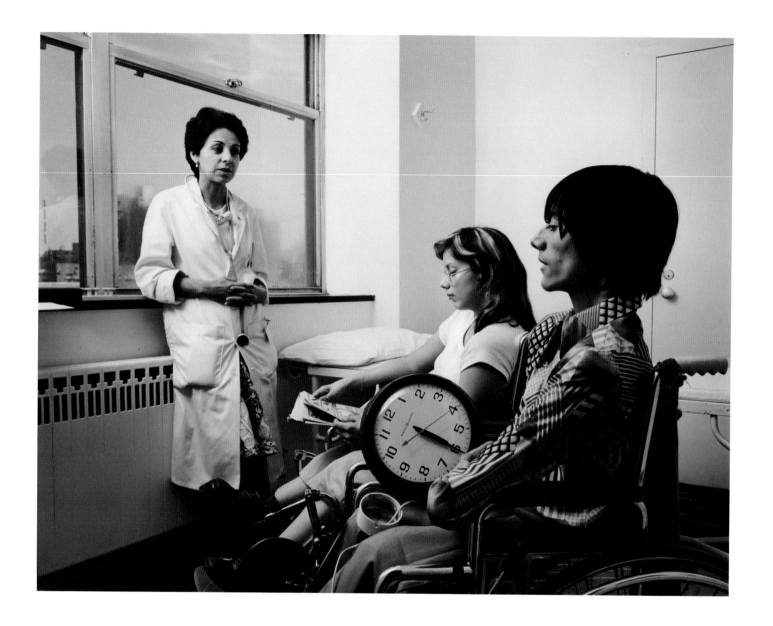

The Art of the Portrait

James Borcoman

Since the fifteenth century, portraiture has endeavoured to interpret the messages that lie in the human face, the breach that betrays the motions of the mind. Portraiture has been seen sometimes as a metaphor to express the artist's own emotional state, sometimes as a symbol of universal human qualities. This book and the exhibition to which it relates stress the need to distinguish between the portrait as a physiognomical map only and its more profound implications. But the art of portraiture begins with the establishment of physical fact as the basis for our knowledge of spiritual fact. Without knowledge of the surface, we cannot know the essence. Therein lies the portraitist's constant pursuit: the search for meaning in appearances.

No pictorial medium has equalled photography in its zeal to pay close attention to the surface detail of the world. And no medium has done so with such ambivalence, for, as photographer Garry Winogrand has said, there is nothing so mysterious as a fact clearly described.[1] It is this ambivalence that also poses the greatest challenge for the viewer: to go beyond the fact into the mystery and, if not to penetrate it, at least to confront it.

Yousuf Karsh has built a world-wide reputation as a photographer of famous persons. Many of his portraits stand as icons of twentieth century humanity. What is less well known is the other side of his career – the many thousands of more ordinary folk who have passed before his lens. In these photographs lies an unexpected richness, hidden from view until the National Archives of Canada acquired his entire collection of prints and negatives in 1987. A description of this important archive may be found in Lilly Koltun's essay "The Karsh Collection." Now that it is available for exploration, this unknown side of Karsh will receive fuller examination in coming years.

However, Karsh's avowed purpose has been to capture for posterity the faces of those individuals he feels have shaped the twentieth century, in the scientific, political, and cultural arenas. Therefore, the core of the exhibition and book has been given over to just that, albeit with portraits less well known and some that have neither been published nor exhibited. The smaller portion of the exhibition represents the work that made the studio economically viable, and is divided loosely into two groups: studio portraits and photographs made on assignment.

To understand the nature of Karsh's imagery it is important to place his work in context. Philip Pocock's essay, "The Portraitist at Work," analyses the social and cultural influences on Karsh. Estelle Jussim's essay, "The Psychological Portrait," places his work in the context of a view of portraiture that has existed since Leonardo da Vinci and discusses what has been, perhaps, the single most powerful theme in the history of the photographic portrait.

65

Fig. 1
David Octavius Hill (Scottish, 1802–70)
and Robert Adamson (Scottish,
1821–48)
Henry Dunlop 1843?
Salted paper print
20.5 × 14.7 cm
National Gallery of Canada, 31254

The following essay presents examples of certain key developments in the history of the photographic portrait, each chosen with special reference to Karsh's œuvre, in order to help locate him within the mainstream of the genre. Each is related to a crucial turning point in his career.

Interlude: Credibility and Communion

The world's first photographic portrait was made, so it is believed, by Alfred Donné on 14 October 1839, almost two months after the first public demonstration of the daguerreotype in Paris. The first photographic studio was opened by Alexander Wolcott and John Johnson in New York by the beginning of March 1840. Since then, over the one hundred and fifty years of its existence, photography's principal enterprise has been the portrait.

At the beginning, both the negative-positive paper process invented by England's William Henry Fox Talbot, and the daguerreotype process that was the brain-child of France's Louis Jacques Mandé Daguerre, may have been seen essentially as scientific pursuits. Both processes, however, soon became of equal interest to the artistic community. It was as natural a step for Hermann Biow, for instance, to add the new picture-making method to his skills as portrait painter by opening Hamburg's first daguerreotype studio in 1841 as it was for landscape painter David Octavius Hill to adopt Talbot's process when he embarked in May 1843 on his project of recording the faces of all those who had participated in the founding of the Free Church of Scotland. Through trained painters such as these, the photographic portrait became a continuation of a long artistic tradition, as much concerned with the æsthetic quality of the image as with the accurate recording of physiognomy. Photography, however, added an ingredient hitherto absent from the painted portrait – credibility.

And something perhaps even more important, a sense of communion with the original object.

The Victorian imagination was captivated by what was seen as a special relationship between these two ideas – credibility and communion – and the principal means by which the photographic portrait was made. "The picture is connected with its prototype by sensibilities peculiarly touching," wrote the Scottish scientist David Brewster in the *Edinburgh Review*, January 1843. "It was the very light that radiated from his brow – the identical gleam which lighted up his eye – the pallid hue which hung upon his cheek – that pencilled the cherished image, and fixed themselves for ever there."[2]

The studio that D.O. Hill opened in partnership with the young photographer Robert Adamson at Rock House on Calton Hill in Edinburgh in the summer of 1843 became the setting for hundreds of portraits of Edinburgh society and of almost every famous visitor to the city over the next four-and-a-half years. When they made their portrait of Henry Dunlop, Lord Provost of Glasgow (fig. 1), possibly in 1843, their purpose was twofold: to show the physiognomy of a particular individual who had been involved in an event of historic importance (the establishing of the Free Church) and to symbolize the power of a man capable of momentous deeds.

Hill and Adamson's search for character through the use of a strong top light on the sitter's head and hands is a direct inheritance from Henry Raeburn and the tradition of Scottish portrait painting. As a pictorial device, its purpose is to enliven the surface of the picture and at the same time serve a symbolic end. The broad planes of the face, emphasized by an uncompromising light, suggest a strong and rugged character. The concentration of the brightest highlight on the forehead creates a luminous and heroic brow. Dunlop's great dome of a forehead becomes a magnificent symbol of power, both intellectual and physical.

Such qualities are emphasized by the ability of the paper negative and the salted paper print to suppress local surface information in favour of breadth of form. Known as the "broad" or the "general effect," it was a pictorial concept widely discussed by theorists in the nineteenth century. The basis of a picture, they argued, consists of broad masses of light and dark areas in opposition to each other as a means of defining the general character of the subject and directing the thrust of the composition. Art, said Joshua Reynolds, consists in "the power of generalizing; and in the shortness and simplicity of the means employed."[3]

Karsh: The Crafting of Beauty

The causal texture of art is rich and varied. Undoubtedly the most difficult to discern are the influences that are rooted in childhood. Although Yousuf Karsh has emphasized the poverty of his childhood in a community devoid of any artistic environment, Armenia in fact has a rich cultural heritage in architecture and the visual arts. Remnants of mosaics and frescoes, and especially illuminated manuscripts, from the Middle Ages and the seventeenth century, show a richness and diversity of ornamental design. Karsh's maternal grandfather was a gold engraver, and his two uncles were calligraphers and illuminators. The child had opportunity to be aware not only of beautiful objects, but of the role that raw materials have in the crafting of beauty.

The first influences that can be established with any certainty, however, are those to which Karsh was submitted in John Garo's studio. These were profound and lasting. In the year 1928, when the youthful Karsh arrived in Boston to begin his apprenticeship with Garo, photographic portraiture still seemed to be inextricably caught in the coils of the pictorialist movement that had been

Fig. 2
Yousuf Karsh
John H. Garo 1931
Gelatin silver, printed later
26.7 × 31.6 cm
National Archives of Canada, PA-165838

born at the end of the nineteenth century. Soft focus, atmospheric effects, and romantic idealism dominated the fashionable studios. The sharp objectivity of the modern movement, characterized by the work of such photographers as the Americans Edward Weston, Edward Steichen, Alfred Stieglitz (all former pictorialists), and Paul Strand, and the Europeans Lucia Moholy and August Sander, had as yet had little impact.

As early as 1914, Garo had an established reputation for being able to bring out the character of a sitter, for the richness and subtlety of his work, and especially for his skilful control of printing processes.[4] Garo taught Karsh how to see his subject in terms of light, shadow, and form, and to understand that light is the photographer's greatest gift. Karsh's portrait of Garo made shortly before leaving his master's employ in 1931 shows the complexity for which the young photographer was already striving (fig. 2). Light gives life to the texture and soft folds of the smock Garo wears in a manner that forecasts things to come.

By the mid-1930s, Karsh's use of light has become more assured. With his portrait of actress Ruth Draper, made in his Ottawa studio, he flamboyantly declares his mastery over light (pl. 2). Light is his theme. It suffuses the drapery with a soft glow that gives a concrete presence to both the sitter and the cloth and at the same time makes the space around the figure almost palpable.

In his portrait of B.K. Sandwell, editor of *Saturday Night*, made several years later, light serves the more utilitarian object of modelling the sitter's head and giving shape to the personality, but Karsh cannot resist also using it for a more playful purpose (fig. 3). The counterpoint between the white highlight slashing through the dark space at the bottom of the picture and the muted tones of the rhythmical curve at the right adds a graphic touch both witty and decorative.

Fig. 3
Yousuf Karsh
B.K. Sandwell 22 March 1939
Gelatin silver, printed later
37.8 × 32.9 cm
National Archives of Canada, PA-165840

69

Fig. 4
Hermann Carl Eduard Biewend
(German, 1814–88)
Myself, with Little Luise on My Lap,
Hamburg 4 June 1850
Daguerreotype with applied colour
15.7 × 10.3 cm (sight)
National Gallery of Canada
Gift of Phyllis Lambert, Montreal

From Garo, Karsh learned not only the more common printing processes, but also the techniques of bromoil, platinum, and gum-bichromate printing. He learned that each of the photographic papers used in these methods has its own individual quality of beauty. During the years that Karsh acted as Garo's apprentice, and subsequently for some months as his printer, he came to understand how to exploit the character of a given photographic paper, to make it part of the expressive quality of the portrait. And perhaps he even came to feel, albeit unconsciously, a certain appreciation for the print in terms of the decorative qualities of the illuminator's art as practised by his two uncles before their untimely deaths while he was still a child.

70

Interlude: Eduard Biewend

By the time the gifted amateur photographer Eduard Biewend had made his daguerreotype, *Myself with Little Luise on My Lap* (fig. 4) in 1850, certain rules about photographic portraiture had been laid down. Among other requirements, the sitter must never look directly at the camera lens, but a little above or to one side, in order to avoid "a fixed, silly, staring, scowling or painful expression."[5] But it is, of course, precisely the smouldering intensity of Biewend's direct stare that makes his portrait so powerful. The force of the expression in both face and hands communicates a grasping for eternity – always implicit in the enterprise of portraiture – and a fierce parental love.

Biewend was a scientist employed as Master of the Mint at the Bank of Hamburg in Germany. It is not known whether he had any artistic training. The pose in his self-portrait is straightforward and without artistic pretension and in several ways quite typical of many daguerreotypes – seated, half-length, frontal, with the sitter presented in an anonymous space. Except for the dark, vertical band at the left, there is no formal tension in the image. The tension is entirely psychological, the result of the projection of a distinctive presence. The eye contact with the viewer transmits a message about the human condition.

The sharp delineation of the sitter, the precise rendering of the qualities and textures of the clothing, the distinctness of every hair on the child's head, have made this image both sensually beautiful and compellingly true. Biewend has seen acutely. Literal description is given æsthetic form. Hill's portrait of Henry Dunlop and Biewend's self-portrait may represent opposing schools of artistic thought, yet neither detracts from the beauty of the other.

Karsh: Lighting

After his three years with Garo, the next significant stage in Karsh's development was the discovery that artificial studio light could liberate the photographer from the restrictive hours of daylight and offer a new freedom. At the time, the traditional light source for portraiture was daylight, and Garo's Boston studio used it exclusively. After he opened his own studio in Ottawa, Karsh carried on Garo's methods for a time.

The turning point occurred, however, with his introduction to the Ottawa Little Theatre in the autumn of 1932. Only recently arrived in Ottawa, where he was employed as an assistant in John Powis's studio on Sparks Street for the first few months, he was invited to watch rehearsals at the theatre. Impressed with the inventive manner in which the director used stage lighting, he saw immediately the possibilities for his own work. He was given the opportunity to experiment when the Ottawa Little Theatre asked him to make publicity photographs.

Some of the dominant elements in Karsh's style have their beginnings in the theatrical studies of this period. In *Saint Joan*, a scene from the George Bernard Shaw play, photographed in the mid-1930s, we witness the use of carefully studied lighting to establish mood and effect and to reinforce the structure of the composition (fig. 5). Highlights are used to delineate form against broad dark spaces. A face, a figure, a hand, carefully modelled by light, emerge from shadowy depths. Drama is established by the opposition between darks and lights. Stillness, certainly the result of Karsh's studied control, creates an atmosphere of timelessness, as though the subject is carved in stone. We are not participants in a fleeting incident in the passage of time but recipients of a moment distilled out of time,

Fig. 5
Yousuf Karsh
Ottawa Little Theatre: "Saint Joan"
18 November 1936
Gelatin silver print (emulsion-texture-enhanced)
30.4 × 22.9 cm
National Archives of Canada, PA-165843

imbued with a special significance by the photographer, presented for our eternal contemplation. Some photographers dissect the flux of time, Karsh monumentalizes it.

Interlude: Étienne Carjat

Charles Baudelaire, author of *Les fleurs du mal*, is France's most notorious nineteenth-century poet. Étienne Carjat has given us one of the most unremittingly truthful portraits in the history of photographic portraiture, a masterpiece of its genre, the image of a bitterly disillusioned man. Even if we have never heard of Baudelaire, we recognize the terrible beauty and power of the force that lies within this face (fig. 6).

Carjat, like his contemporary Nadar, concentrated on photographing the French cultural and social élite during the approximately fourteen years (c. 1861–76) that he operated a studio. Undoubtedly his skills as a caricaturist made him uncommonly sensitive to the essential and most telling attributes of his sitters.

In his portrait of Baudelaire, Carjat shows us, with utmost economy and simplicity, the face of a driven genius. Nothing is allowed to compete with the presence of the sitter. The eyes make direct contact with the viewer so forcefully that we are momentarily stunned. The vitality of the image is intensified by the simple manner in which the shoulder at the left of the picture falls out of focus – as though powered by a life force that cannot be constrained.

Some fifteen years after this portrait was made, it was published as a woodburytype print in the *Galerie contemporaine, littéraire, artistique*. Launched in 1876, and published serially for eight years, the *Galerie contemporaine* consisted of portfolios of photographs of the great men and women in literature, art, music, science, and politics of France, made by some of the most

Fig. 6
Étienne Carjat (French, 1828–1906)
Charles Baudelaire c. 1863
Woodburytype
23.1 × 18.2 cm
National Gallery of Canada, 32781.143
From *La Galerie contemporaine* (1878)

celebrated portrait photographers of Paris, including Nadar, Pierre Petit, and Adam-Salomon. Each portrait was accompanied by a three-to-four-page biographical text. It was the most elaborate attempt yet to satisfy, through photography, the public's insatiable hunger for likenesses of celebrities.

Karsh: *Winston Churchill*

The third turning point in Karsh's career was his photograph of Winston Churchill (frontispiece), not only Karsh's best known portrait but undoubtedly the one by which Churchill is best remembered. While with Garo, Karsh obviously had enjoyed the heady atmosphere created by the constant stream of celebrities and creative personalities that flowed through the studio. He made the early decision that people such as these, who mark their era, would become the subject of his camera.

It was an ambition that Karsh tried to instill in his new employer, John Powis, shortly after joining his studio in Ottawa. In the autumn of 1932 the Imperial Economic Conference was held in that city. Here was a heaven-sent opportunity to photograph well-known people. A number of heads of state were to attend, among them Neville Chamberlain, the British Prime Minister. Reluctantly, Powis allowed himself to be convinced, but although Chamberlain and others accepted invitations to be photographed, the resulting portraits by Powis created little sensation.[6]

As experience, however, the exercise had been worthwhile. Over the ensuing years, once Karsh was on his own, similar opportunities to establish a portfolio of eminent personalities were taken – in the first instance, by photographing those members of the local community to whom he was most drawn, its creative people – the artists, poets, writers, actors, and musicians. Then, in

73

1935, because he knew their son, Lord Duncannon, through his association with the Ottawa Little Theatre, he was invited to make official portraits of Lord Bessborough, the Governor General of Canada, and Lady Bessborough. The portraits appeared in *The Illustrated London News*, *The Tatler*, and *The Sketch*. His career was launched.

The 1930s were the years in which Karsh was establishing his reputation within the photographic community. Beginning in 1934 with the National Gallery of Canada's first Canadian International Salon of Photographic Art, and every year thereafter until its demise in 1939, Karsh had prints accepted in this prestigious exhibition, which included work by Margaret Bourke-White, Pierre Dubreuil, Frank Fraprie, Alexander Keighley, and Leonard Misonne, among others. In 1936, he exhibited in the London Salon of Photography, held in the quarters of the Royal Society of Painters in Water-Colours. Two years later, he was elected an associate member of the Royal Photographic Society. In 1940, *Photograms of the Year*, the British-based arbiter of international photographic taste since the turn of the century, began to reproduce his work (fig. 7).

It was the Churchill portrait, however, that rocketed him to the heights of international renown. Three elements contributed to the success of this image: skill, luck, and insight. Karsh's lighting, patiently organized with a stand-in the night before in a corner of the room where the portrait was to be made, is reminiscent of Hill and Adamson's portrait of Dunlop. It was arranged to place the emphasis upon Churchill's head, turning it into a metaphor for power, intellectual force, heroic strength and canny wisdom. Even the back-lighting that creates a glow on the panelled wall behind Churchill's head serves not only to bring the space around the subject to life, but also to reinforce the symbol of glowing power.

Fig. 7
Yousuf Karsh
The Lesson before 1940
Matte gelatin silver print
41.8 × 33.4 cm
Collection of the artist

Comparison with a portrait made nine years earlier by Steichen shows a slightly younger Churchill in an almost similar pose and with an expression on his face remarkably close to that in Karsh's photograph – and also with a dark suit, bow tie, and watchchain. In both, Churchill appears as a forceful personality, but in the Karsh portrait this quality is strengthened by direct and unrelenting eye contact with the viewer and by the shadow that models his face at the left and outlines it against the lighter background. Both these elements, not there in the Steichen photograph, speak of an unyielding nature.

There is no doubt that Karsh was presented with an extraordinary piece of luck when Churchill continued to puff on a cigar after taking his designated place for the portrait. But there was more than luck in Karsh's reaction to the moment. Recognizing, in the first instance, that the big cigar was an inappropriate accessory for this world leader, and then, after his instinctive snatching away of the cigar, perceiving that the resulting expression of belligerence on Churchill's face offered the right moment to make the exposure – that was the act of genius. A second exposure made after Churchill had recovered his composure shows a slightly smiling, almost cherubic man – the portrait his family preferred, but not the one that became the famous symbol of lion-hearted determination in the face of evil aggression.

The Churchill portrait was widely published immediately after it was made, including an appearance on the cover of *Life*. It has been exhibited over the years in many formats, including the monumental size of 60 × 40 inches. Each printing expresses the monolithic nature of the symbol, but in none does this appear to greater advantage than in a small print on 14 × 11 inch paper made much later. Unfortunately, no print of the Churchill from the early period has come to light, so it is difficult to know for a certainty how Karsh interpreted his negative at the beginning.

Over the years, Karsh has periodically changed the interpretation of his negatives through printing. The image of Grey Owl, which began life as an almost full-length figure, was reprinted from the same negative around 1963 as only a detail of the face negative (pl. 7). The early printings of Jean-Louis Barrault are precise, with a defined space in the background, sharply modelled face and hands, and a chairback glistening with the tactile reality of hard varnish. The 1988 printing (pl. 13), on matte paper, shows us a more mysterious and romantic Barrault emerging from a smoky, atmospheric background, and a chairback that has been reduced to its linear elements.

Although Karsh did not continue the use of bromoil, gum, or platinum printing that he had learned in Garo's studio, he frequently printed on matte silver papers, his favourite being an emulsion-texture-enhanced paper with a scratchy tooth to the surface almost like fine sandpaper, commonly referred to in the trade as having a suede finish, and manufactured under the name Opal V. This surface results in deep, warm, matte blacks that seem to recede into the paper, in an extraordinarily subtle range of middle tones and creamy highlights that glow from the depths.

Unfortunately, these papers ceased to be manufactured in the 1960s, but before he used up the last of his stock, Karsh printed the Churchill on this paper, and with wondrous results. The rough surface of the paper marries perfectly with the craggy face and skin texture, hiding none of its detail. The tonal depths in the shadow areas of the figure seem to have no limit, suggesting a mysterious presence. Against the deep blacks, the glint of the metal watchchain and the glow of the luminous and softly modulated white shirt and handkerchief are counterpoints that add both credibility and a subtly decorative beauty to the image.

Then we notice, in his pocket, the envelope or folded paper with the same subtly modulated

Fig. 8
Julia Margaret Cameron (British, 1815–79)
Alethia (Alice Liddell) 1872
Albumen silver print
32.4 × 23.7 cm
National Gallery of Canada, 21285

white surface, and we are faced with the accidental, the human touch, and the minor mystery. What did this great man so hastily jam into his pocket as to crinkle the edges of the paper? We shall never know but forever remain intrigued.

Interlude: Julia Margaret Cameron

Approximately ten years after Carjat made his portrait of Baudelaire and six years before it was published, Julia Margaret Cameron photographed Alice Liddell (fig. 8). We seldom think of the heroine of *Alice in Wonderland* as a grown woman. Here she is, however, the person for whom as a young girl Lewis Carroll had written his stories.

Self-taught, an amateur in the true sense of the word, Cameron began to photograph only in middle age. Professional photographers found her technique clumsy. Images were out of focus. Subjects moved during exposure. Her photographs lacked the crisp finish of the professional studio. Cameron was, in fact, the greatest innovator in nineteenth-century photographic portraiture. Her emphasis upon the dramatic close-up, rather than the usual three-quarter or half-length view, represented a radical departure. More than that, her out-of-focus technique, stumbled on either by accident or design, became the basis for the pictorialist school that began to flourish at the end of the nineteenth century. As with Hill and Adamson, her purpose was to emphasize form and character through the broad effect, a quality she

76

achieved by means of lighting and throwing much of her subject out of focus.

We are surrounded by things, as Kenneth Clark has said, with a different life and structure to our own. The artist's purpose is often to find a meaningful harmony between ourselves and the world in which we live. Cameron frequently gave to her portraits allegorical titles to draw our attention to the presence of deeper meanings in her images. To her portrait of Alice she has given the title *Alethia*, after the goddess of fruit trees. It is an apt title, reflecting as it does the symbolic union between the foliage and Alice's long hair, flowing in waves from the tangled branches.

The role that the photographic print has played in this bonding is important. It lies in the process of abstraction. The artist who is sensitive to the materials of the craft will instinctively understand that the properties of these physical substances make possible the translation from one level of meaning to another. The tones of the hair and the leaves in *Alethia*, for instance, are united by the warm tones of albumen silver in the print, thus turning a mirror image of reality into a moving and mysterious statement about that reality.

Karsh: Words and Images

The next significant turning point in Karsh's career occurred in 1946 with the publication of his first book, *Faces of Destiny*. Following his success with the Churchill portrait, he made a concerted effort to gather material for an international collection of renowned leaders. Many of the people he most admired at that moment in history "were all under one roof, in London, England, all the exiled heads of Europe, all the men of letters and science. Everyone had volunteered to do his part. I wanted this," said Karsh, "the men and women who were the saviours of our civilisation."[7] He made a list and showed it to his friend Prime Minister Mackenzie King, who furnished a letter of recommendation and opened the door to the Canadian High Commission in London.

Provided with an advance by *Saturday Night* to cover his travel expenses, Karsh set sail from Halifax at the end of summer 1943. Between 12 September and 12 November, he photographed forty-two celebrities, including King George VI, King Haakon of Norway, Field Marshal Smuts, Lord Beaverbrook, Lord Louis Mountbatten, H.G. Wells, George Bernard Shaw, and Noël Coward.

The portraits were immediately published serially in *The Illustrated London News*. Upon his return to Ottawa he held an exhibition of the entire group in the Drawing Room of the Chateau Laurier Hotel. Much to his surprise, the public lined up to see it.

The success of this venture resulted in an assignment from *Life* to photograph some seventy dignitaries in Washington during the months of March through May 1944. In the following year, during April and May, he photographed for *Life* the delegates to the San Francisco Conference, the founding meeting for the United Nations. With these three trips, he now had enough material for his first book.

It could be argued that *Faces of Destiny* was following in the footsteps of the *Galerie contemporaine*, some seventy years later. In a broad sense the same formula was applied. A full-page portrait of a celebrated artistic, literary, or political figure was accompanied by a text with information about the sitter. Here the similarity ends. *Galerie contemporaine* contained photographs from a number of sources. The texts, by a variety of authors, had nothing to do with the photographers. When Karsh made his 1943 trip to England, his first wife, Solange, made him promise to record his experiences with the sitter immediately after each portrait session. On subsequent trips, she accompanied him to help perform this duty. These notes provide the basis for the

Fig. 9
Yousuf Karsh
W.H. Auden 30 October 1972
Matte gelatin silver, printed 1988
27.5 × 19.8 cm
National Gallery of Canada
Gift of the artist

personal reminiscences that accompany the portraits.

In an essay written in 1952 on the relationship between words and photographs, Nancy Newhall discussed the idea of photographs accompanied by words – photograph/text – as a form of communication separate from either alone.[8] In order to distinguish the function of the title (which identifies the subject or theme) and that of the caption (which provides a minimal set of facts that usually cannot stand alone) from that of the text, she explained that the latter, "no matter how closely related to the photographs, is a complete and independent statement . . . ." In other words, two separate statements, one visual, the other literary, are juxtaposed, each extending the content of the other and together making a third statement.

The reader looking at *Faces of Destiny*, or Karsh's subsequent books, must pay as close attention to the words as to the photographs in order to understand the extended statement. This is the key to the insights for which Karsh is searching, "the essence of the extraordinary person."[9] On the one hand, we have the carefully posed and studied formality of a Karsh photo-graph, on the other there is the informality of the text. We are told in intimate but elegant prose what occurred during the sitting, what the photographer and his subject discussed, how each responded to the portrait session. But the photo-graph can never tell the whole story, or perhaps not the story the photographer wants it to tell.

Words come to the rescue, either to enhance the legend that surrounds the sitter, or to add the human dimension that places the viewer on more intimate terms with the legend. According to John Pope-Hennessy, "Portraiture is the depiction of the individual in his own character."[10] And if the photograph gives us a face that masks the character, or if it portrays no more than a partial truth, what then? "In a sense," Karsh explains,

78

"physiognomy can belie personality, and I would be the first to admit this."[11]

We have only to look at the photograph of blind, deaf, and mute Helen Keller and her friend Polly Thomson and read the text that describes the sitting in *Karsh Portraits*[12] to understand both the extent to which he has used the word-photograph relationship to breathe a special humanity into the portrait, and the immense appeal this has for the public. To read the following words, as another example, beside the portrait of poet W.H. Auden, standing wistfully in the gloom of his friend Stephen Spender's tangled garden (fig. 9), is to experience a kind of tragedy only hinted at in the photograph: "He spent two hours talking to my wife – prophetically – about friends who had died. He smoked incessantly, his conversation punctuated with wracking coughs. Meanwhile the light had gone from the garden, and I could take only a quick photograph of a beautiful and ravaged face. 'Come soon, come soon,' he invited, but I knew I would never see him again."[13] This is not to claim that a verbal accompaniment is mandatory, but only to emphasize that Karsh has used this form in his books to advantage and that such a presentation is of a different order to that of the exhibition print that stands alone.

A case in point is the portrait of the Duchess of Windsor made in 1971, but never used in any of the books (pl. 49). Here the visual language of the photograph operates powerfully in its own way by making metaphoric allusions and provoking questions rather than by providing answers directed by a text. Undoubtedly one of Karsh's strongest portraits, it is an example of how skilfully he can combine æsthetic form with expressive content. The woman who would have been Queen of England is seated in a regal pose on a throne-like chair. The formal elements all conspire to create an image of beauty, full of grace and symmetry. The heart-shaped curve of her head is repeated in the curves of the chair that

shine with an aura of light. The diaphanous material of her costume reflects a suffused glow, giving it a quality of misty gossamer.

Karsh has exploited the subtle greys of the paper on which the image has been printed to give it a shimmer, creating a cloud of dusty silver about the sitter's form. This is a modern gelatin silver paper with its own special qualities, which Karsh has exploited to the fullest. It is continuing evidence of his sensuous response to the materials of the craft.

But within the grace and symmetry of Karsh's photograph we are also strongly aware of discordant psychological elements. The Duchess of Windsor's face contrasts dramatically with the seductive folds of the drapery. There is a paradox here that speaks of harshness and at the same time of sadness, of power, and of fragility. She has been pierced with a wistful mortality.

Interlude: August Sander

Pictorialism was in vogue among art photographers from the end of the nineteenth century well into the 1930s. With its roots in Julia Margaret Cameron's out-of-focus portraits, it was promoted by P.H. Emerson in England, Robert Demachy in France, and Stieglitz through his Photo-Secession movement in America. In portraiture it emphasized the broad effect and suppressed surface information, as may be seen in such examples as Coburn's *Gertrude Käsebier* (see fig. 17) or Carter's *Fantasy* (see fig. 23). Often the pictorialist employed the "Rembrandt effect," a term used to describe the dramatic opposition of light and dark for the purpose of suggesting mood or character. The figure emerges from shadow in a glow of light, or certain parts of the figure are swallowed up by shadows that are outlined by a glow of light from behind.

One of the earliest photographers to break away from the prevailing style of pictorialism was

79

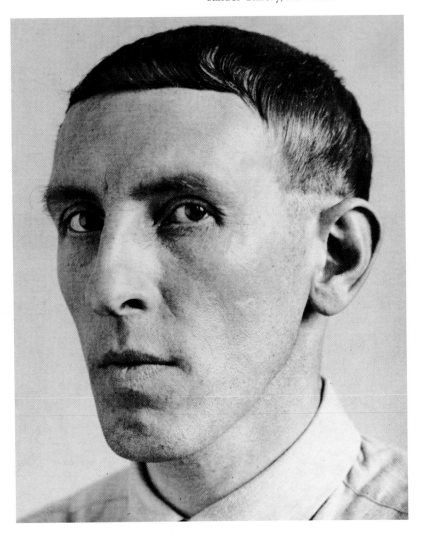

Fig. 10
August Sander (German, 1876–1964)
Heinrich Hoerle 1928
Gelatin silver print
61.0 × 48.4 cm
Sander Gallery, New York

August Sander. His description of a typical studio of the turn of the century, in which the photographer used painted Italianate scenery, movable balustrades, and Rembrandt lighting to transform "a kitchen maid into an elegant lady and a simple soldier into a general,"[14] no doubt reflected his own approach in the early years. In 1910, he opened a studio in Cologne, renouncing the prevailing vogue by advertising that he would make "simple, natural portraits that show subjects in an environment corresponding to their own individuality, portraits that claim the right to be evaluated as works of art . . . ."[15]

Sander was one of the first of his generation to understand that photography had an æsthetic of its own, based upon a clear depiction of literal fact. This clinical vision may be seen to have its roots in the daguerreotype. Between the self-portrait by Biewend (see fig. 4) and Sander's portrait of his friend, the painter Heinrich Hoerle (fig. 10), there is an obvious parallel. Both are simple in formal terms, rely upon precise definition, and are psychologically expressive. Hoerle's level gaze is marked by the projection of a distinctive presence, a presence that has turned to inspect us with a directness that is disconcerting.

The simplicity of the formal elements underlines the psychological content. Sander's uncompromising examination of Hoerle's face, far from adhering to the conventional idea of attractiveness, emphasizes its massive, bony structure and the linearity of its features — hair, eyes, ears, mouth, and jaw. But it is precisely this that gives the portrait its æsthetic validity.

Powerful as the Hoerle portrait is in its own right, in association with the body of Sander's work there is a subtext containing wider implications. About the time he moved to Cologne, Sander conceived the idea of assembling a large series of portraits, in groups, to project an image of his time. His goal was to reveal how the collective power of human society produces

80

common types of appearances. His eye extracted patterns of social class and cultural levels to establish similarities. Using photographs selected from his studio work, commissioned portraits, and portraits made for passports and identification cards, among other reasons, as well as from personal work made specifically for the project "Man in the Twentieth Century," he published his first version in 1929 as *Face of Our Time*. By grouping images, Sander established archetypes to define the characteristics of humankind in general. He found the universal in the particular. Although we may disagree with his philosophy, he has made nevertheless a statement about humanity that is challenging, revealing, and moving.

Karsh: The Subtext

Some of the most compelling images in the history of photography are of unknown people or of individuals whose importance has long been forgotten. The hunger we have for physiognomy does not stop with the famous but derives from a deeper need – to identify with humanity itself. If the portrait of Biewend (see fig. 4) is as powerful as that of Baudelaire (see fig. 6) or of Churchill (frontispiece), it is because the force of the sitter's personality is communicated directly to us. But more than that, it is a measure of the extent to which the photographer has seen and given form to his or her observations, thus guiding our eyes and shaping our minds.

Clarity, precision, plainness, directness – a priest in traditional ecclesiastical vestments, Karsh's *Paul Bernier* presents both a lyric and a complex mystery (fig. 11). The subject of this portrait was not a public celebrity. He was one of those who came to the studio because someone other than Karsh wanted the portrait. We must remember that the bulk of Karsh's work consists of this kind of commission, providing the economic basis for the studio. Despite the fact that

Fig. 11
Yousuf Karsh
Paul Bernier 23 August 1952
Gelatin silver print
34.4 × 26.6 cm
National Archives of Canada, PA-165844

81

Fig. 12
Yousuf Karsh
Donald B. Anderson 21 April 1964
Gelatin silver print (emulsion-texture-enhanced)
32.8 × 25.5 cm
National Archives of Canada, PA-165845

the portrait of Bernier was not intended for a portfolio of the famous, Karsh as always has given full attention to his subject. The quality of that attention is seen in his sensitivity to the sitter. Receptive to the priest's open and honest face, he has shown us an individual who has the appearance of being strong and capable at the same time as he is warm and caring. And perhaps, because he is human, a touch vulnerable.

Karsh has seen these attributes in both the body language and the frank and honest gaze of his sitter. He has astutely avoided the more conventional poses that allow a sitter to assume positions that mask the private self in order to create a contrived public image.

A number of Karsh's portraits of professional people – doctors, lawyers, and clergy – made during the last several decades present their subjects standing, three-quarter length, in a frontal pose and a neutral environment, in a sense naked to the camera. The subjects must accommodate themselves to an anonymous space, and the resulting body language becomes Karsh's key to interpretation. In *Paul Bernier*, the stance of the body, the gesture of the hand, the tilt of the head, the expression of the face, the texture of cloth, are all part of a text to be read.

The impulse behind much of Karsh's work is, in a sense, philosophical, and stems from a belief in the dignity, goodness, and genius of human beings. The particular reality he captures with the camera is the symbol of this faith. Often he augments this symbol through the insertion of lesser symbols. We are told that Paul Bernier is a priest through the simple device of his clothing. But what is Karsh telling us about Donald Anderson (fig. 12)? In the first instance, the compass that Anderson holds is a tool used by engineers and architects. At an elementary level, therefore, we learn that he is a man who builds or designs. In fact, he is the executive of an oil company in New Mexico.

There are other levels of meaning in this image, however, that are difficult to ignore. The compass has a long history of symbolism in art, signifying the act of creation. Being related to the letter A in its simpler design, the compass also stands for the beginning of things. The aggressive contrast between the metallic geometry of the compass and the swirling, amorphous background reinforces the idea of creation out of chaos. What makes the portrait of Anderson especially compelling is the manner in which the head, dominating the space, acts as a point of stability. The sitter's expression, with its direct gaze, seems to challenge us to either assert or deny the act of creation.

Sometimes, as with the portrait of Anderson, or with Karsh's better-known portrait of the novelist Vladimir Nabokov holding a butterfly, the symbol takes a predominant place in the composition. One of the most amusing and complex examples of this type may be found in *Man Ray* (pl. 34), in which the larger portion of the image is taken over by Man Ray's own self-portrait. At other times, the symbol is introduced more subtly, as in the portrait of the doctor Leon Charash (pl. 48). Here, the relationship between the book's title and its author's body language is especially poignant.

There are times when the accidental presence of certain elements, unseen by the photographer at the time of the exposure, may take on a symbolic role in the final image. It is a phenomenon peculiar to photography, as though we discover the meaning of the world only through the photograph. One of the most disquieting examples is to be found in the portrait of Robert Oppenheimer (pl. 19). When we know of Oppenheimer's involvement in the production of the atom bomb and suspect the implications of the messages on the blackboard behind him, the discovery of the little notice that says DO NOT ERASE takes on an alarming significance. In

another example, it is perhaps fitting that, in Robertson Davies's environment, the camera should have witnessed the presence of the contrasting symbols of the spirit and the flesh at the left of the portrait (pl. 41). Or, what are we to make of the shadowy figure on horseback (Napoleon-like) in the background of the portrait of the former mayor of Montreal, Camillien Houde (pl. 20), or of the clock in a photograph from the muscular dystrophy series (pl. 46)? The presence of such an object poses questions that augment the meaning of the piece, opening up levels of interpretation.

There are other ways in which the meaning of a photograph may be extended. Photography's expressive purpose is often best achieved through the juxtaposing of two or more images. August Sander used this potential in a controlled way to document his preconceptions about humanity in the twentieth century. But the photographer's meaning may not always be apparent at the time of release of the shutter. By drawing relationships between certain photographs and juxtaposing them into groups, hidden messages will emerge. In such instances, the whole is greater than the sum of its parts, and a new or deeper experience is moulded for the viewer.

Application of this approach to work made on assignment, alluded to at the beginning of this essay, reveals a side to Karsh not hitherto explored. The portraits of Emilio Pucci (pl. 50), Joseph Schaffner (fig. 13), and Louis Quarles (pl. 51) were each taken separately with no intended relationship. The addition of two more to the group – portraits of Edmond Joly de Lotbinière and A.J. Major – also taken separately, is instructive. Each is a fine portrait in its own right, ultimately given distinction by Karsh's sensibility. Each shows a diversity of expression and a variety of visual invention. The de Lotbinière portrait is a simple close-up of a youngish man in profile against a neutral background. Pucci stands in a

Fig. 13
Yousuf Karsh
Joseph Schaffner 17 June 1970
Gelatin silver print (emulsion-texture-
enhanced)
19.0 × 22.2 cm
National Archives of Canada, PA-165841

frontal pose resting his arm on a cabinet; behind him, an elongated archway glowing with light completes the image of elegance. Schaffner sits at his desk looking away from the camera, surrounded by his prized possessions. Quarles faces the camera in close-up, wearing a yachtsman's cap, the billowing sails of a model boat behind him. Major stands with his arms folded, frontally, head slightly tilted, glancing downward.

Each shows us a separate aspect of humanity. When brought together, however, a subtext emerges. The comparisons sharpen the meaning of each expression and, at the same time, contribute to a level of meaning about humankind. De Lotbinière's youthful confidence and optimism contrast with the determination of the older man that we see mirrored in Pucci's face, a man perhaps at the peak of his career, still driven by an energetic force, and not yielding an inch before our scrutiny. Schaffner, much older, his struggles and achievements in the past, shows us a contemplative individual whose gaze is inward. Quarles gives us a direct stare, softened with age, the challenge is gone, and we see a man of advanced years facing us with equanimity. Finally, the portrait of Major, who seems imprisoned within the vertical forms of the split background, is of a man whose wistful glance perhaps dwells upon a sad daydream. The subtext of the group presents us with a gentle but perceptive observation of humanity.

These are not portraits of celebrities. They are portraits that celebrate humanity. By grouping individual photographs together we move from the particular to the universal. It is as though, with the immense body of Karsh's work, accumulated over six decades of time, we look out over a vast landscape of faces that shapes a larger and more eternal theme.

Physiognomy outlives ourselves and ends not in the grave.

— Thomas Browne (1605–82)

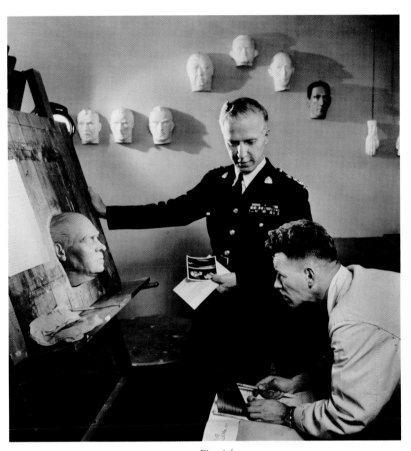

Fig. 14
Yousuf Karsh
Commissioner L.H. Nichols with sculptor Cpl J.R. Abbott of the identification branch, R.C.M.P. Headquarters, Ottawa 1952
Gelatin silver print
20.9 × 19.4 cm
National Archives of Canada, PA-165846
For the *Maclean's* assignment "Face of Canada"

Notes

1. Ben Lifson, "The Carpentry of Pictures," *The Village Voice* (15 January 1979).

2. [David Brewster], "Photogenic Drawing, or Drawing by the Agency of Light," *The Edinburgh Review*, 154 (January 1843), p. 331.

3. Joshua Reynolds, "Eleventh Discourse" (10 December 1782), *Fifteen Discourses Delivered in the Royal Academy* (London: J.M. Dent, 1906, reprint 1928), p. 177.

4. A.J. Philpott, "John H. Garo – A Study and an Estimate," *Wilson's Photographic Magazine*, LI:6 (June 1914), pp. 253-61.

5. Henry H. Snelling, *The History and Practice of the Art of Photography* (New York: G.P. Putnam, 1849), p. 41.

6. Yousuf Karsh, *In Search of Greatness: Reflections of Yousuf Karsh* (Toronto: University of Toronto Press, 1962), p. 41.

7. Taped interview between the author and Yousuf Karsh, Ottawa, 7 and 8 December 1988.

8. Nancy Newhall, "The Caption: The Mutual Relation of Words/Photographs," *Aperture*, 1 (1952).

9. Karsh, *In Search of Greatness*, p. 189.

10. John Pope-Hennessy, *The Portrait in the Renaissance* (New York: Bollingen Foundation, 1966), p. xi.

11. Karsh, *In Search of Greatness*, p. 102.

12. Yousuf Karsh, *Karsh: A Fifty-Year Retrospective* (Toronto: University of Toronto Press, 1983), p. 69.

13. Karsh, *A Fifty-Year Retrospective*, p. 67.

14. August Sander, "The Nature and Development of Photography," Lecture 3, quoted in Robert Kramer, *August Sander, Photographs of an Epoch, 1904–1959* (Philadelphia: Philadelphia Museum of Art, 1980), p. 16.

15. Sander, advertising brochure, c. 1910, quoted in Kramer, p. 17.

The Psychological Portrait

Estelle Jussim

On African safari in 1954, Ernest Hemingway, his wife Mary, and the pilot of a small plane, found themselves in mortal danger. The plane had briefly lifted off, crashed down, and burst into flames. Mary and the pilot escaped through a window, but Hemingway was too large to follow them. He battered his way out through a twisted metal door by repeatedly slamming his head against it. According to one of his biographers, Hemingway suffered a fractured skull out of which the very brain fluid dripped, two spinal discs were crushed, a kidney and his spleen ruptured, and his face, arms and head were burned.[1] The media portrayed him as triumphant over his injuries. Miraculously, not only had Hemingway physically survived, but his reputation as a macho hero was greatly enhanced. By coincidence, this was the year that he won the Nobel Prize for literature.

But Hemingway was not intact. He had been seriously injured, the physical destruction having led directly to psychological impairment of such magnitude that he could no longer write to his own satisfaction. He talked of failure and suicide. This was assiduously kept from the public, although everyone seemed to know that he was again drinking heavily. In 1957, *Life* magazine invited an autobiographical essay by Hemingway, and commissioned Yousuf Karsh to photograph the literary lion in his den. Karsh obligingly flew down to Cuba. The visit of a few days was cordial, although Karsh later noted that the writer was one of the shyest men he had ever met. Hemingway posed for a few informal pictures in which he could be seen smiling, drinking, and relaxing. Then Karsh set up his equipment and lights and the great portrait of Hemingway (pl. 25) was accomplished.

In 1961, two weeks before Ernest Hemingway killed himself with a double-barrelled shotgun held to his head, Mary telephoned Karsh. Presumably she did not say that she feared Hemingway's imminent suicide. Hemingway had been in and out of the Mayo Clinic and had been receiving electroshock therapy for acute depression and threats of suicide, and she probably felt she could not talk about this without somehow compromising her husband. What she did tell Karsh was that the 1957 portrait was Hemingway's favourite. Would Karsh release that portrait to the press and to the public as often as possible? Would he show it to as many people as possible? It was if she wanted to ensure her husband's favourable image.

For all we know, the 1957 Karsh portrait may not have been Hemingway's favourite, but rather his wife's. Without knowing specifically what attributes of self the famous author had wanted to display, his wife's request seems to indicate that she, at least, saw in the portrait a chance for Hemingway to be understood, forgiven his sins, loved. The portrait seemed to present Hemingway indicating, "Here I am, this is what I am, this is the way you should remember me." And remember

87

him thus we do, for the Karsh portrait manages to convey not only a suffering human being, but the dignity of that person, the epitome of what Hemingway believed was the noblest virtue: grace in adversity.

As we study the portrait, how much of our reading of it depends on what we already know of Hemingway? How much, on the leather-fronted sweater, resembling as it does the buckler of a knight in armor who has just removed his helmet? On the dramatic lighting that renders his bristling beard and mustache in tactile detail? On his tense, well-lined forehead, the deepset eyes curiously lacking in expression, the crow's-feet descending like tears from the lower eyelids – all physiognomic signs of what most of us believe are universal indicators of character and emotion? We may try to answer these questions; we may also want to consider our emotional response to the portrait and to the background and context of its place in the iconography of Hemingway.

If you had known nothing of Hemingway, had not read this recounting of the plane crash, his injuries and his psychological failure, would your reactions to the Karsh portrait have been different? Any fair assessment of what has been called the "psychological portrait" demands that we recognize our pre-knowledge of the subject. That appears to be the most elementary level of interpretation, for many much more complex issues emerge from what would seem to be a simple act: looking at a portrait.

For example, even if we already suspect that no portrait is a completely reliable representation of the sitter's personality and character, do we believe that it is possible to unmask the sitter to reveal the "true" self to be discovered? Do we stop to consider if there is actually only *one* "true" self to be discovered? And can we safely ignore the photographer's preconceptions and æsthetic and social ideology as these influence what is clearly a commercial and cultural transaction? Before

addressing these interrelated issues, it might be wise to investigate the reliability as well as the validity of physiognomic interpretation, since we first seek answers from the visual clues in any photographic portrait.

It has long been assumed that the expression of the face, the gesture and posture of the body, the clothes and personal ornaments, and even the context of a portrait can reveal profundities of character, personality, and emotion. We did not have to wait until the age of Freud to interpret the portrait this way. Socrates was recorded as saying, "Nobility and dignity, self-abasement and servility, prudence and understanding, insolence and vulgarity, are reflected in the face and in the attitudes of the body whether still or in motion."[2] Freud, who was looking for clues to abnormal psychology, noted that it was impossible to disguise these reflections. "He that has eyes to see and ears to hear may convince himself that no mortal can keep a secret. If his lips are silent, he chatters with his fingertips; betrayal oozes out of him at every pore."[3] Supposedly, then, the face is the mirror of the soul, while the body is the gossip revealing all. What is also implied is that clues revealed by face and body are intelligible to all humans by a kind of physiognomic universal language. The gestures of an aborigine, the face of a prime minister, could be read by anyone, in any culture, anywhere.

Not even the eighteenth-century creator of the physiognomic science, Johann Kaspar Lavater, was so rash as to insist upon total universality or on complete transparency of face and body. In his *Essays on Physiognomy*, published starting in 1772, the Swiss clergyman, who wanted to demonstrate that the Divine Spirit resided in all humankind, wrote that physiognomy was "the real and visible expression of internal qualities, which are themselves invisible."[4] Admitting that a person's social rank, general condition and apparel could obscure those internal qualities, Lavater nevertheless hoped to discover fixed and scientifically accurate principles by which to judge qualities of character. Unable to explain by what methods he determined the alphabet of his proposed universal language of nature, Lavater failed to persuade the public of the correctness of his analysis. He did, however, successfully establish the theory that facial and bodily clues constituted a form of language of character.

If face and body revealed attributes of internal psychological truths, then it was presumed that photography could capture these revelations and record them for posterity. During the nineteenth century, photography was equated with optical certitude, a science of fact. Thus, when Charles Darwin came to write *The Expression of the Emotions in Man and Animals* in 1872, he turned to photography for the accurate and reliable record of his subjects that the traditional graphic arts could not supply. Darwin, too, was trying to discover if there were universal principles or a universal language of emotional expression. In his preparations, he made note of several challenges for photographic portraitists: "The study of Expression is difficult, owing to the movements being often extremely slight, and of a fleeting nature. . . . When we witness any deep emotion, our sympathy is so strongly excited, that close observation is forgotten or rendered almost impossible."[5] Furthermore, there was an unsuspected barrier to correct interpretation – imagination – for if one expects to see any expression, it is all too easy to imagine its presence. Darwin suggested that, in all honesty, it was difficult to determine with certainty the movements of the features and of the body that we tend to identify with certain states of the mind. Nevertheless, he sustained his investigations until he could offer the conclusion that certain facial expressions and body postures were innate and therefore universal, while others were apparently learned. These careful observations were considered inflamma-

tory at the time because Darwin was persuasive in linking human expressive states to those of the great primates.

Darwin's work on expression was primarily concerned with whether or not "the same expressions and gestures prevail, as has often been asserted without much evidence, with all the races of mankind, especially with those who have associated but little with Europeans."[6] He did note, for example, that one of his correspondents in India was having difficulty obtaining photographs of the natives that were of any use in answering this major question "owing to their habitual concealment of all emotions in the presence of Europeans."[7] Why this simple fact did not deter him from making assertions about the universality and genetic origins of human expression is difficult to understand. The question of whether we are able to decode symbolic expressions from one society to the next has never been resolved to anyone's complete satisfaction and remains in the background of our response to portraiture.

Many photographers, however, continue to insist that they possess an instinctual power of photographic interpretation. This is the problem that confronts anyone seeking illumination on the subject of the "psychological portrait." For which psychology is it – that of the subject, or of the photographer, or of both? Do photographic portraitists keenly observe their subjects, or do they keenly project their own psychological attributes and expectations onto their subjects? Or do the two in combination inevitably cloud any discussion of the photographic portrait? As Susan Sontag remarked emphatically, "photographs, which cannot themselves explain anything, are inexhaustible invitations to deduction, speculation, and fantasy."[8] Diane Arbus concurred: "A photograph is a secret about a secret. The more it tells you the less you know."[9] Are the great portrait photographers deluding themselves when they talk about

89

Fig. 15
Napoleon Sarony (American, b. Canada,
1821–96)
Oscar Wilde 1882
Albumen silver print
30.4 × 18.4 cm
Library of Congress, Washington

possessing a gift that enables them to portray a subject's true self?

To carry the discussion further, it seems crucial to define the essential elements of portraiture. For the moment at least, let us accept the idea that a portrait is first and foremost a picture of someone who has deliberately posed for the photographer. The idea of posing is crucial. The subject of the portrait is presenting a dramatic facade, enacting a moment of personal theatre, perhaps even inventing a persona for the sake of portrait. Thus, we begin looking at a photographic portrait with that assumption of self-dramatization, then go on to examine the physiognomy of the poser, the total body gesture of the pose, the facial expression, the hair-style, the clothing and miscellany like eye-glasses and jewellery, the way that chiaroscuro is handled, and finally, the formal arrangement of shapes within the containing frame (usually rectangular, but often oval or round), since this influences mood. These factors are all intrinsic to the picture.

When we start to consider the era in which the portrait was produced, several other factors influence any response. These are not just the historical costume, which may serve as an indication of a period piece, but the pose as a result of photographic expectations of the time, the studio accoutrements, the handling of natural as opposed to artificial light, the speed of the emulsion and length of the exposure, the orthochromicity of black-and-white films, the truth to nature of colour films, the size of the print – all these are of interest as well.

Not to be overlooked is the fact that commercial photographers are paid for their work. Ordinarily, the sitter pays the operator. This has been true except for the great celebrities of the nineteenth century, who leased their images to studio photographers for a fee. Oscar Wilde, on tour in the United States in 1882, was paid royalties for the distribution of his image in

90

"æsthetic dress" – long hair, velvet jacket and breeches – as portrayed by Sarony (fig. 15). Wilde's visit coincided with the U.S. run of Gilbert and Sullivan's *Iolanthe*, in which he was caricatured as a foppish poet. During this visit he was in fact seriously proselytizing the æsthetic theories of William Morris.

In general, we should never forget to ask for what purpose a particular portrait was made: for a *carte-de-visite* advertisement? – for a reproduction in *Life* magazine? – for a memento in a college yearbook? – for the frontispiece of a book by the sitter? – as a reminder of family on the desk of a corporate executive? Or perhaps the portrait is intended as a fine art object to be exhibited in galleries? – as publicity for a new movie? – as the glorification for posterity of a president or prime minister? Surely the ultimate use of the photograph (although portraits may have more than one use), depending as it does on who or what agency is paying for it, should enter into our interpretation of the psychological presentation of the sitter.

To be paid for a portrait places a peculiar restriction on a photographer: the need to please the payer. In some cases, it is the publication that must be pleased; in others, it is the sitter; in still others, it is both. At the same time, the individualism and the photographic technology of the twentieth century have freed portrait photographers to impose their personal styles upon their subjects. These styles range from the dominant abstract shapes used by Arnold Newman in his 1950s portrait of Igor Stravinsky, by which the composer was made to appear as a tiny appendage to a grand piano, to the appalling naturalistic detail of Richard Avedon's larger-than-life-size pictures of his aged father. The imposing of such personal pictorial styles seems to contradict the photographers' avowal that they seek only the soul of the sitter.

Gertrude Käsebier was a noted turn-of-the-century portraitist who hoped for the ability to

Fig. 16
Gertrude Käsebier (American, 1852–1926)
Miss N (Evelyn Nesbit) c. 1902
Platinum print
20.5 × 15.6 cm
National Gallery of Canada, 31391

make true photographic biographies. In her portrait of Evelyn Nesbit (fig. 16) – the mistress of the architect Stanford White, who was later murdered by her husband – Käsebier managed to convey Nesbit's luxuriant sexiness, the invitation in her posture that seems to speak of a readiness to capitulate, and simultaneously, a trace of voluptuous *tristesse* on her lovely face. In fact, instead of beckoning the viewer to sexual adventure, Nesbit's body speaks of an infinite world-weariness calculated to stop any arousal. Which was the true Nesbit, the willing courtesan or the tired young woman? Which did Käsebier believe she was photographing? If we are to accept Käsebier's reputation, we should believe that she saw both aspects of Evelyn Nesbit and responded accordingly.

As for Gertrude Käsebier herself as a subject for psychological portraiture, Alvin Langdon Coburn photographed her (fig. 17) when he was an assistant and associate in her portrait studio for a few years at the beginning of his career. In several portraits he made of her wearing the accessories shown here, she seems to be nervously pulling on a string of beads obscured beneath a decorative scarf. Was she symbolically trying to strangle herself? Her eyes seem wary, but they are essentially unreadable because the pupils are drilled out by a bright studio light. Pulled back slightly, as if leaning against the tension of the beads she clutches so firmly, her head supports a weighty hat that matches the decorations of the twisted scarf. We cannot be sure if she is trying to essay a fleeting smile. The young photographer, later such a master of the portrait, here was apparently more interested in the design of scarf, hat, darks, lights, and repeated circles, than in a careful study of her face. Certainly the grasp of the beads indicates nervous tension, and if she was not unfriendly she was at least aloof.

Such an interpretation matches what is known about her during the first ten years of this century.

Fig. 17
Alvin Langdon Coburn (British, b. U.S., 1882–1966)
Gertrude Käsebier 1903
Gum-bichromate and platinum print
26.9 × 21.1 cm
International Museum of Photography at George Eastman House, Rochester

She was repeatedly on the verge of nervous exhaustion, writing to friends like F. Holland Day that she was unable to cope with her landlord, or bear the strained relations with Alfred Stieglitz – who was chastizing her for her commercial work, without which he did not seem to realize she could not have supported herself. Whether or not Coburn had been listening to her troubles, and had therefore determined to reveal her psychological tensions in her portrait, he succeeded in capturing a distraught but proud woman.

Any interpretation of Käsebier's soul would have to take into account several earlier self-portraits she made in which she appears to be a healthy, well-adjusted, successful career woman, all smiles and self-confidence. The particular moment in a person's life at which a portrait is taken obviously will influence our perception of character. What may be true at one instant may be misleading at another.

In her own day, Evelyn Nesbit was a celebrity, just as Gertrude Käsebier was in a more limited circle. Even before the murder of Stanford White, Nesbit was constantly in the newspapers. Her portrait by Rudolf Eickemeyer in 1902, which showed her draped in a loose kimono and lying on an immense polar-bear rug, was every bit as notorious as the poster of the nude Marilyn Monroe fifty years later. Yousuf Karsh is only one of many photographers who have devoted themselves to portraits of the famous, if not, in his case perhaps, the notorious.

There is more than just idle voyeurism in the desire to examine the faces of celebrities. As Ben Maddow observed about our enchantment with such people, we are driven by the twin emotions of admiration and envy. Maddow likens humans to a "claque of monkeys or a posse of coyotes, groups with whom we share the common trait of sociability,"[10] and who all have leaders, decision-makers, activists, even criminals – the equivalent of our celebrities. Maddow sees us as having a distinct behavioural need to group ourselves around leaders. Sometimes the leaders have admirable traits, but sometimes their only virtue is notoriety. According to Maddow, it doesn't much matter which. We read eagerly about these people, we watch them on television and film. Whatever they do – run for political office, invent rockets, cure fatal diseases, marry princes, purchase million-dollar houses, give lavish masquerade parties on the Riviera, engage in illicit affairs – we are fascinated. In turn, it is our interest which perpetuates their fame. Is it possible to interpret a portrait of one of these scintillating and very public characters as being "psychological" – a true portrait, that is, of the person's psyche? Will the celebrity not always be posing – playing a role?

Karsh would have us believe that it is possible to make such true portraits: "All I know is that within every man and woman a secret is hidden, and as a photographer it is my task to reveal it if I can. The revelation, if it comes at all, will come in a small fraction of a second with an unconscious gesture, a gleam of the eye, a brief lifting of the mask that all humans wear to conceal their innermost selves from the world. In that fleeting interval of opportunity the photographer must act or lose his prize."[11] It is a remarkable task that Karsh sets himself, especially since so many of his most famous subjects have had vast experience in maintaining that mask. Winston Churchill (frontispiece) no less than Artur Rubinstein knew very well how to present himself, Churchill in his bravura role of indomitable leader, Rubinstein in the grand manner of the musical genius posed almost as if bowing to an unseen audience. Andy Warhol, Tennessee Williams, Sophia Loren, Tyrone Power, John Fitzgerald Kennedy, George Bernard Shaw, Laurence Olivier, Vivien Leigh, Joan Crawford, Ingrid Bergman, Humphrey Bogart – all of

93

the famous names Karsh has photographed present equally famous public faces in most encounters. The miracle is that Karsh has managed so often to charm his sitters into – however brief, however partial – a relaxing of the mask.

For those who know Karsh only as a photographer of the well-known, it is somewhat of a surprise that he also has taken portraits of the anonymous individuals in the streets of the many countries he has visited (fig. 18). These are more in the style of the snapshot than of the seriously posed studio portrait.

A photographer who did make carefully posed and powerfully composed portraits of people who weren't public figures was Walker Evans. We confront a very different sort of person in his familiar portrait of Floyd Burroughs (fig. 19). Burroughs was a cotton sharecropper living in Hale County, Alabama, and there in 1936 Walker Evans took a series of portraits of him and his family. To say that they were dirt poor is an understatement. Yet these people had an inherent dignity despite their flour-sack dresses and bare feet. The Floyd Burroughs we see here, unshaven, in a dusty overall and mended shirt, is a human being who refuses to lie down and surrender to life's inequities. Squinting into the hot sun, his grey eyes staring, his mouth quiet, and the posture of his body indicating someone who could get up to do a hard day's work, Burroughs is a strong person whose elfin ears enhance his inherent good looks. There is puzzlement, too, in his face, and a deep sense of sorrow. We should remember that he was posing for a well-educated, well-off New Englander, and this may have affected his pose, as any portrait is affected by the relationship between photographer and subject.

Evans took another picture in 1936 that can help indicate what features reveal socio-economic status as well as the psychological make-up of a subject. An unidentified landowner from Moundville, Alabama, stands before us (fig. 20). He wears an ill-fitting jacket with sleeves much too long, rumpled, unpressed, catching him in the left armpit. One suspects he hastily put on a tie and hurried into the first jacket he could find. With his slack posture, the way in which he is crammed visually against the implacable horizontals of the clapboard, and his frontal pose, he resembles a prisoner posing for a mug shot. He may be a landowner, but he is not wealthy by plantation standards. His face is tense but resolute, his eyes narrowed, his ears sticking out like the proverbial jug handles, his white hair disappearing into the background. Here is a man who has no pride of position, nor even pride in self. Evans accords him no sympathy. He is not granted the dignity evinced by Floyd Burroughs. His clothes especially make him ludicrous. He is without grace or distinction.

94

Fig. 18
Yousuf Karsh
Quebec City 1953
Gelatin silver print
11.0 × 10.9 cm
National Archives of Canada, PA-165847

Fig. 19
Walker Evans (American, 1903–75)
Floyd Burroughs, A Cotton
Sharecropper, Hale County,
Alabama Summer 1936
Gelatin silver, printed 1988
23.7 × 18.8 cm
Library of Congress, Washington,
LC-USF342-8138

95

Fig. 20
Walker Evans (American, 1903–75)
Landowner, Moundville,
Alabama Summer 1936
Gelatin silver, printed 1988
23.6 × 18.6 cm
Library of Congress, Washington,
LC-USF342-8127

Fig. 21
Edward Steichen (American,
1879–1973)
Solitude (F. Holland Day) 1901
Photogravure
12.1 × 16.1 cm
International Museum of Photography at
George Eastman House, Rochester
Published in *Camera Work* LV:33 (April
1906)

Clothes do, in fact, often make the man – and woman – in photography. One of the finest portraits ever taken by Edward Steichen was hidden away in *Camera Work* with its famous subject unidentified. The title given was *Solitude*, and the sitter was the pictorialist photographer and Boston publisher, F. Holland Day (fig. 21). The shadow of a large, handsome beret obscures his right eye, giving his left eye the mysterious stare of someone in hiding. His smoking jacket, if such it is, would appear to be of velvet. On his elegantly placed hand he wears a substantial pearl ring, with the ring finger juxtaposed to his sensual mouth and well-trimmed mustache and beard. If Day had been wearing an undershirt, fedora, and school

96

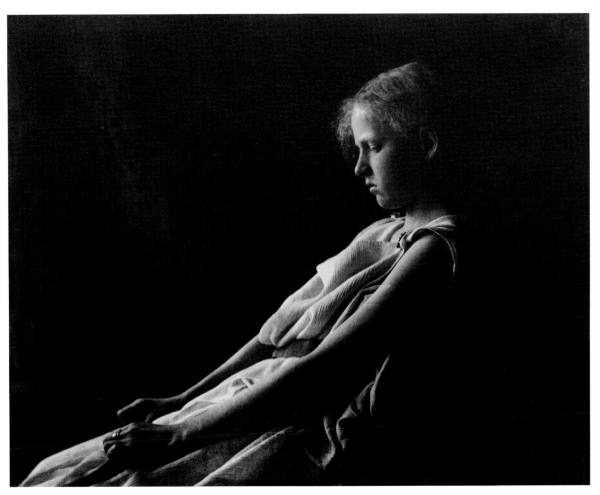

Fig. 22
F. Holland Day (American, 1864–1933)
Tow-headed Girl in Chiton c. 1897
Platinum print
18.5 × 23.2 cm
Library of Congress, Washington

ring, Steichen might not have photographed him, and we would not have been granted this insight into a wealthy and proud but lonely artist.

The chiton, hair-style and rings would seem to place one of F. Holland Day's younger sitters (fig. 22) in the upper economic stratum, but we cannot be sure of the correctness of that opinion. Day often dressed his subjects in costumes. The seriousness of the girl's face, with her lips slightly parted, the tension in her hands and the thrust of her neck, together seem to indicate that she is not entirely at ease posing for the photographer. The beautifully balanced composition indicates that the photographer was completely in charge of the pose and the lighting, so we cannot trust such a photograph to deliver any psychological insights other than into the æsthetic ideology of F. Holland Day. Is it quite accurate to call such a picture a *portrait* of the sitter?

The same question applies to the lovely photograph by Sidney Carter called *Fantasy* (fig. 23). Surely we can tell immediately that this kind of picture was not intended to capture the soul of the sitter. We might be willing to hazard the guess that the young woman caressing a wooden Japanese creature could never turn into a similar monster. She seems too tender, almost amorous, this Beauty holding her Beast with her left hand clasped to a frontage of peacock feathers. Yet whether she was a professional model or a close personal friend of the photographer's we will probably never know. Her true soul remains an enigma. All that is clear is that Sidney Carter found her a suitable subject for a fantasy of his own.

Investigators into the meaning of nonverbal communication agree that clothing is an important indicator of more than socio-economic status. It can function as "decoration, protection (both physical protection and psychological protection), sexual attraction, self-assertion, self-denial, concealment, group identification, and display of status or role."[12] Occupation, nationality, relation to opposite sex, official status, mood, personality, attitude, interests and values may all be indicated, with many of these attributes being communicated simultaneously. Take for example Anne Noggle's striking portrait of her friend Yolanda (fig. 24): here is an aging woman who insists on dressing well and looking attractive. The firm placement of her fuzzy beret, the silver earrings, the well-polished nails, the jaunty cigarette, the attention-catching striped turtleneck and the dark smooth coat are all psychological and social indicators as telling as her hawk-like eye, her wrinkled skin, her tight lips. A bohemian? An

Fig. 23
Sidney Carter (Canadian, 1880–1956)
Fantasy 1921
Gelatin silver print
24.3 × 19.2 cm
National Archives of Canada, PA-112013

98

artist? Something about this woman speaks of idiosyncrasy, independence and a dramatic flair barely held in check by her grip on that cigarette. And by no means is she poor.

What Noggle does in her ongoing portrait series is to force viewers to confront their prejudices and fears about aging. "To look straight into a face and find the pulse of what it is to be human"[13] is the fuel for her creativity. When she photographs older women, she focusses "on the tension between the iron determinant of age and the individual character of the subject."[14] Her ambition is not simply to explore that character, but to make a significant statement about what happens as we are betrayed by age, our still valiant spirit increasingly dimmed by the passage of years. To call Noggle's portraits "psychological" is only half the story. She offers philosophical insights about the human condition and empathy for those who show stubborn determination not to submit to the cultural notion that age equals decrepitude. The portrait of Yolanda epitomizes Noggle's fierce yet sympathetic approach to personality.

Yolanda lived in Santa Fe, not far from the Abiquiu of Georgia O'Keeffe. In 1956, before O'Keeffe had attracted quite the amount of media attention that she did in later years, for example at her recent posthumous exhibition at New York's Metropolitan Museum of Art, Yousuf Karsh took one of his finest portraits of a woman artist (pl. 37). With her famous hands in full view, dressed as always in black, her hair swept tightly into a small bun, O'Keeffe is seated in a room that demonstrates her customary austerity. Whitened tree stump beside her, and overhead the gigantic skull and antlers of a stag – one of her favourite painting subjects – O'Keeffe gazes quietly toward a patch of sunlight at her door. The averted gaze with its thoughtful smile cannot hide the power implicit in her arms and hands.

In one of the pictures Karsh took during his visit, O'Keeffe posed her hands in a position made

Fig. 24
Anne Noggle (American, b. 1922)
Yolanda 1983
Gelatin silver print
24.0 × 16.1 cm
Collection of the artist

famous by her husband, Alfred Stieglitz, who took no fewer than five hundred portraits of her over a ten-year period. But it was not only Stieglitz's infatuation with his intriguing genius of a wife that caused him to produce so many portraits of her. He knew a single photograph could never capture her infinite variety. As Edward Steichen noted, "it has sometimes been said of the work of certain portrait painters that, by prolonged study and work with the model, they were able to produce a synthesis of the sitter's complete personality. But here we must remember that it took great writers like Balzac or Proust volumes to bring us a living portrait of a person. To imagine that a visual artist in any medium could condense a complete portrait into one picture is putting a strain on logic."[15]

It might be worth pausing for a moment to reconsider what we mean by the "psychological portrait." Are all portraits not psychological in some way? There are portraits in which people present themselves for posterity; they act out the part of their dream persona, and they are always handsomer than usual: Sarony's Oscar Wilde (see fig. 15) fits. Then there are portraits in which people subject themselves to the staring eye of the camera and submit to being made into documents of social conditions: Walker Evans's portrait of Floyd Burroughs (see fig. 19), for instance. There are also portraits in which individuals can be seen posing as if for dramatic tableaux – the photographer's imagination superimposed on human flesh: Sidney Carter's *Fantasy* (see fig. 23) is a good example. There are portraits in which individuals let us know they are playing a role not just for the photographer, but for us, the viewers: Edward Steichen's *Solitude* (see fig. 21) might be in that class. There are also photojournalistic pictures of two or more people, often married couples – pictures in which the viewer is expected to see revelations of private aspects of the relationship, especially, perhaps, dissension

and repressed anger. Among the most infamous of this latter category are the shots of Marilyn Monroe and her husband, the playwright Arthur Miller, on the set of their film *The Misfits*. Their privacy once invaded, they were perhaps so unhappy that they did not care what the photographer noticed or recorded. Celebrities become so used to playing out their lives in front of cameras that maybe in time they can no longer differentiate enough between the pose and the person to protect themselves from such displays.

The controversial poet Ezra Pound was in no position to protect himself from public scrutiny when, at the end of World War II, he was incarcerated as a treasonous madman who had made broadcasts for the Fascists. A legendary figure in pre-World War I England, friend to Wyndham Lewis, Alvin Langdon Coburn and the Vorticist group of painters and writers, Pound's flamboyant red hair, cape and beret had been instantly recognizable anywhere. When Henri Cartier-Bresson photographed him shortly before his death, however, he seemed a ghostly, tormented vision (fig. 25). A wrinkled, rumpled old man, with eyes glaring hate and rage, his hair standing on end, his hands knotted on his lap, Pound resembled a psychopath more than the one-time leader of the Imagist poets. Does he evoke pity? Perhaps. The criss-crosses of his wrinkled forehead speak of anguish. Perhaps. We know that his obsessive, outrageous anti-Semitism was only one side of his politics. Kind writers and artists kept him out of jail by insisting on his madness as opposed to his treason. Cartier-Bresson, with characteristic brilliance, encapsulated both the violence and the suffering in one unforgettable image.

Richard Avedon insists that portraits reveal little but the photographer's own penchants and beliefs. "A portrait is not a likeness. The moment an emotion or fact is transformed into a photograph it is no longer a fact but an opinion. There is no

100

such thing as inaccuracy in a photograph. All photographs are accurate. None of them is the truth."[16] If we agree with such a vehement statement, we are forced to question other photographers who claim they are seekers after the truth. For Avedon insists that "a portrait photographer depends upon another person to complete his picture. The subject imagined, which in a sense is me, must be discovered in someone else willing to take part in a fiction he cannot possibly know about."[17]

Surely Avedon did not mean that we should believe the portraits in his exhibition *In the American West* contain his own imagined self. Those portraits of carnies, oil workers, stone cutters, rodeo hands, waitresses, are over life-size. Does he see himself as superhuman? Each figure is isolated against a seamless white studio paper that Avedon carried around various cities in the vastness of the West, along with studio equipment and a number of assistants. Does Avedon envision his soul as isolated for inspection? In his merciless portraits of Isak Dinesen, Truman Capote, Dwight D. Eisenhower – emphasizing the frailties of each – did Avedon create fictions so repugnant that he reveals himself as a self-hater, an everybody-hater, in fact?

When the critic Harold Rosenberg wrote his essay, "Portraits: A Meditation on Likeness," he remarked about Avedon that the photographer recognized the performance aspect of the portrait-making event. Sitters want to get across to potential viewers some conception of themselves. But, noted Rosenberg, "The portraitist. . . has his own vision of the person before him, and his authenticity as an artist and as an individual depends on embodying this image in his picture. Thus a conflict arises between the portraitist and his subject – not merely the resistance of the material that is experienced as art, but a battle of human wills and imaginations. . . ."[18]

Fig. 25
Henri Cartier-Bresson (French, b. 1908)
Ezra Pound 1971
Gelatin silver print
24.2 × 16.1 cm
Magnum Photos, New York

Fig. 26
Arnold Newman (American, b. 1918)
Alfred Stieglitz and Georgia O'Keeffe 1944
Gelatin silver print
24.1 × 19.4 cm
National Gallery of Canada, 32322
Gift of Dorothy Meigs Eidlitz, St. Andrews, New Brunswick

Nowhere is this conflict better epitomized than in Arnold Newman's double portrait of Alfred Stieglitz and Georgia O'Keeffe (fig. 26). Arnold Newman has widely recognized æsthetic intentions, and, as Philippe Halsman remarked, Newman began as an artist and continued as a photographer (Halsman is inadvertently excluding photography from "art") who tries to make formally decorative and symbolic compositions.

As is evident from Newman's picture, Stieglitz was a sick old man in the 1940s. He was still highly regarded as the father of modern photography and as a kind of saint of modern art. The truth was that his wife, here posed as subsidiary and subservient to the presumed genius of her husband, was one of the strongest influences on Alfred Stieglitz and a major force in his life for modernism and abstraction. In trying to avoid the conventional poses of husbands and wives, Newman unfortunately diminished O'Keeffe's true significance. That was perhaps a function of the decade: historians and critics had not yet recognized the extent of O'Keeffe's contributions. Newman was basing his composition on his received image of O'Keeffe and on the reputation of Stieglitz. If there is anything "psychological" about this double portrait, it is more a revelation of Arnold Newman than of his subjects.

The double portrait does raise more complex issues, perhaps, than the image of a single individual. In Vaughn Sills's double portrait of a Georgia family (fig. 27), we are introduced to a husband and wife who have serious mental and physical problems. We may suspect such problems from their expressions and their physiognomies, without being able to be certain of their causes. In fact, he was an alcoholic who died a year or so after this portrait was taken. His wife was a severely disturbed individual, a schizophrenic. She too died shortly afterward. Sills presents them frontally, with powerful compositional resonance in the positions of the arms and hands. The photograph is at the opposite end of the artistic spectrum from the Arnold Newman of Stieglitz and O'Keeffe, not just because these two are a pair of hapless misfortunates without fame or reputation, but because the realism is overpowering. If Newman makes us feel that we should regard his two famous subjects as if they are totem figures, essentially untouchable, Sills gives us straightforward accessibility.

In any double portrait, one of the questions concerns the relationship depicted. Who is the more powerful? Who is in command? Who is contented, unhappy, angry, subdued, resentful, confused? Is there affection between the subjects?

Along with the pioneering work of Edward Hall in such books as *The Silent Language* and *The Hidden Dimension*,[19] which investigate cross-cultural nonverbal communication, a suggested thesaurus of emotions and relationships was developed by Robert Akeret in his book *Photoanalysis*.[20] He cites one example of a grandmother and granddaughter whose amateur portraits were taken a good twelve years apart. In each picture, strong affection is discovered in their hugs and broad grins.

Vaughn Sills has made diary-style portraits of herself and her grandmother (fig. 28) that depict ongoing closeness over the years. As is evident

103

Fig. 27
Vaughn Sills (American, b. Canada 1946)
Lois and Joel Toole 1987
Gelatin silver print
38.1 × 48.3 cm
Collection of the artist

from the writing surrounding the subjects, Sills feels it is impossible to project all the psychological factors in their relationship without help from words. She wants to explain, to enlarge upon, to verify, all those aspects of her grandmother – and for that matter herself and their relationship – that cannot be explicitly divulged in a photograph, although it is clear she tells us a great deal by a collage of images. Unlike our response to portraits of celebrities, we cannot bring to Sills's photographs a pre-judgement composed of snippets of gossip, media interviews, press releases, motion-picture character portrayals, or any other material. Since at this writing the photographer Vaughn Sills is comparatively unknown, we likewise know neither fictions nor

truths about her, unless we happen to know her as a colleague, as I do.

We do know a great deal about Diane Arbus – or think we do. Arbus, like Avedon, was influenced by the German typologist August Sander, who was persuaded that persons revealed themselves in terms of class and occupation. He was not perhaps as interested in individual psychology as in the social implications of a type. In this he was undeniably enmeshed in the racist doctrines that Hitler vehemently espoused. Sander's frontal poses of twin sisters, rural families, labour leaders, urban professionals, and even Nazi S.S. officers, gave Arbus the visual clues to her savage portrayals. As Max Kozloff observed, in Diane Arbus's portraits – of the incongruous king and queen of a

104

Fig. 28
Vaughn Sills (American, b. Canada 1946)
Untitled (grandmother/self) 1986
Gelatin silver print
38.1 × 48.3 cm
Collection of the artist

local ball, of midgets, of transvestites, of the frequently reproduced young flag-carrying rightist – "people were marked by the transparency of their self-delusions and branded by their (often marginal) social status."[21] Avedon's cruelty to his celebrity subjects is matched by Arbus's implacable view of anonymous humanity. Even if we were inclined to grant him sympathy, Arbus permits us none for the callow youth sporting his polemical buttons.

Thus far we have been exploring portraits that are essentially without visual context, with Avedon the perfect example of the photographer who deals almost exclusively with images of isolated, out-of-context individuals. However, there are photographers who insist on including the setting in their character portraits. Bill Brandt is one of the best examples of an artist who believes setting is as important as sitter, specifically for the delineation of personality. Brandt's career began with a close-up portrait of Ezra Pound in 1928, but in his series of literary celebrities that began in 1941 and continued through the following decades, he insisted on placing his subjects within expressive environments. About E.M. Forster, Brandt said that he was "forcibly impressed by the Victorian character of the room in which he sat. A hard print brought out this impression. Details were lost as they were in early Victorian photographs."[22] Cecil Beaton appeared as if on stage in the opening of proscenium curtains, with a stage flood behind him splashing light on a painted set. Dylan Thomas, pint of ale in hand, and visually overwhelmed by his own garish checkered jacket, tie and shirt, sat in a shiny tufted-plastic booth in a bar, a small poster of a sexy lady advertising Schweppes ginger-ale over his shoulder. David Hockney, peering through dark-rimmed glasses, was dominated by one of his theatrical paintings and his book-filled studio.

By no means, however, was Brandt limited to finding suitable indoor ambiences. To portray the introverted painter Francis Bacon, Brandt decided to "convey an impression of the loneliness of a human figure in an outdoor scene. Taking that figure close to the camera and on a path stretching away behind him to a distant horizon intensifies the effect of solitude."[23] Thus Brandt expresses his insistence that the artistic elements of a portrait be used to demonstrate an aspect of a subject's emotional life. Brandt's sitters are dominated by his own vision, as they would be by a painter, and sit, walk or stand in poses entirely of his own creation.

In two portraits she made of the abstract expressionist Morris Graves, Imogen Cunningham was less interested in supplying a context that would identify him as a painter than in showing him as ennobled by a poetic soul. Her 1950 portrait of Graves (fig. 29) placed him within a dappled rocky glade where his sunlit, bearded face was only one of the highlights of the scene. Through light, Cunningham was identifying him with the nature of which Graves was a celebrant. In her later portrait of the artist in 1973, she placed him in a garden, serene, contemplative, with long hair, monkish robe, and hands folded across his abdomen. The two portraits would be nothing without the settings that so perfectly establish mood and tone.

Karsh, too, includes visual context in his portraits of artists like Alberto Giacometti, Josef Albers (pl. 33), Jean-Paul Riopelle, and, of course, Georgia O'Keeffe (pl. 37). Carl Jung sits with his pipe like any writer in his handsome study with its stained glass. The flamboyant Frank Lloyd Wright lurks in the shadowed fastness of Taliesin West amid sculptures, rocks and textured woods. Noël Coward, cigarette in hand, appears with a statuette of a cat that seems to have been a personal icon. Leslie Caron is granted a painting behind her that apparently inspired a hat she was wearing.

Fig. 29
Imogen Cunningham (American,
1883–1976)
Morris Graves 1950
Gelatin silver print
24.5 × 30.3 cm
National Gallery of Canada, 21381

By contrast, Karsh's studio approach just as often favours the strongly lit, more-or-less-isolated face and bust. It is this close-up, dramatically lit imagery that makes many of his portraits seem more like sculptures than photographs. Karsh frequently prefers the backlit profile. In his striking profile of François Mauriac, whom he etched with light, the contour and tactility leap off the page.

There has been criticism of Karsh for his portraits of John F. Kennedy and Martin Luther King, Jr., because they are taken so close to the face of the subject that every pore, hair and facial blemish is recorded. Is this minute detail intended to permit the viewer a glimpse of the souls of these two martyrs? Karsh is so near to his subjects in these portraits that it seems as if he wanted to climb into their heads, the better to understand them. For Karsh, himself a famous man, is obsessed with the great and famous. "The endless fascination of these people for me lies in what I call their inward power. . . . The mask we present to others, and, too often, to ourselves, may lift for only a second – to reveal that power in an unconscious gesture, a raised brow, a surprised response, a moment of repose. *This* is the moment to record."[24] Karsh talks much more about his ability, which he likens to that of a doctor, to see these inward powers, than he does about the environment that might reveal the accuracy of that analysis.

Obviously, Karsh is not alone in believing that it is possible to reveal personality without the aid of information-rich contexts. Edward Weston, too, seemed to think that photographers had the instinctive ability to grasp the character of a sitter in any circumstances. Yet communications specialists argue that "the distinction between what is available for translation and what is actually translated is quite critical. Communication is not continuously and automatically sustained just because people happen to be in each other's presence."[25] Many factors can intervene in face-to-face situations: not everything that occurs is necessarily of significance; the human nervous system can process only a limited amount of information; photographers inevitably project their own ambitions or preconceptions. Karsh, for example, acknowledges that his favourite subjects have been musicians, for "as a group, they tend to be emotional, temperamental, and impatient – and, as a photographer, I thrive on all of these attributes."[26]

Philippe Halsman remarked that Karsh, "with great theatrical flair and technical skill, gets his subjects to act out the image Karsh has of them."[27] If Karsh feels comfortable with musicians, it may be rather that he and they are so similar that recognizing this temperamental closeness permits him to be himself. Halsman was boasting of his own prowess in relaxing subjects with good conversation. Karsh is noted for his ability to charm his sitters with amiable talk. On the other hand, in the absence of evidence to the contrary, one doubts that Richard Avedon would consider conversation as a tool of art.

Like Karsh, Alvin Langdon Coburn was drawn to musicians as well as to famous writers and artists whose pictures were in demand by the literary journals and mass publications. Curiously, his proposed series (never published), to be called *Men of Music*, included not only men but many women, like the young Myra Hess and Wanda Landowska. Coburn's earlier *Men of Mark*,[28] which contained a Picasso-esque portrait of Gertrude Stein, was a collection of images of celebrities using a personalized, modernist approach that made an absolute break with Victorian studio traditions. His portrait of G.K. Chesterton, for example, was notorious for obliterating details in favour of dramatic composition to convey the impression of an enormous talent. Many of his psychologically oriented portraits created a critical uproar, so different were they from conventionally flattering images.

Among Coburn's many portraits of his friend George Bernard Shaw was one taken in 1908 that presented Shaw, for once, in a straightforward intense mood with no twinkling eyes, roguish smile, or hand flirtatiously twisting mustache (fig. 30). Edward Steichen, Coburn himself, and hordes of other portraitists had delineated Shaw as a whimsical clown. Shaw went along with the game, once remarking that he played the outrageous wit because no one would take him seriously. But which would be considered the true psychological portrait of Shaw? Unquestionably he was a

Fig. 30
Alvin Langdon Coburn (British, b. U.S., 1882–1966)
George Bernard Shaw 1908
Photogravure
20.9 × 16.4 cm
National Gallery of Canada
From *Camera Work* XXI:13 (January 1908)

mountebank, a jester, a demonic teller of comic parables; he was also a determined proselytizer for social reform, an essayist, and a critic of acerbic wit and often profound insight. With Shaw such a complex subject, Coburn must have felt that he had no recourse but to take many, many portraits of the playwright. Unlike less fortunate photographers, Coburn had the advantage of long acquaintance with Shaw, as he also did with the sculptor Rodin, whose odd portrait by Coburn, with its off-centre position, flowing beard askew, frowning forehead, and narrowed eyes seemed calculated to annoy studio practitioners of the time.

The changing technologies of camera and film have influenced the ways in which photographers seek to capture psychological truths. With the advent of the 35 mm camera, fast lenses and fast emulsions, photographers could easily snap many moments of presumed truth. Jill Krementz, for example, has been highly successful in her portraits of authors intended for the all-important book jacket. Dancing around her subjects with her small camera, she has caught Tennessee Williams, Janet Flanner, Lillian Hellman, Truman Capote, Studs Terkel, and Susan Sontag in what we are led to believe are characteristic poses. With some, Krementz felt a need to include the telling environment. Others stand alone, filling the frame.

Fortunately or unfortunately, and there are arguments on both sides, the snapshot use of the 35 mm camera (or any of the 6 × 6 cm formats) may encourage us to regard personality as composed of fleeting gestures, evanescent facial expressions and momentary postures. The drama of self-presentation, the formal confrontations with the camera, the carefully studied expression, increasingly give way to the photographer's whim or the accidental revelation. What emerges may be characteristic, but not necessarily *character*. The minutiae of physical habit are not always significant communicators. A legitimate question might be: what more do we actually know of each

108

other than these habitual gestures and expressions? Krementz's pictures argue persuasively that her subjects are revealing their hidden selves. Yet it should be remembered that she is not only seeking psychological truths but is being paid to create images of authors that will sell books. Karsh, too, is a paid professional with the skills needed and used to produce striking front covers for major magazines such as *Life*. His lighting is perfect for good reproduction and for competitive attraction on the newsstand. The studio portraitist may be more concerned with publication than with psychology.

Barbara Norfleet, sociologist, photographer and curator, has maintained a strong interest in the studio portrait. In an essay for one of her compilations, she observed, "The studio photographer must respond to the character, aspirations, and attitudes of his customer if he is to please him. Essential to this task is a knowledge of the iconography, fantasies, and myths of the culture he is visually presenting. He must photograph exactly what his customer takes seriously."[29] Such a statement implies that there is no universal psychological display such as Lavater and Darwin were investigating.

But just how do cultural differences exhibit themselves in a portrait? What aspect of a picture represents what a customer takes seriously? Norfleet's culling of pictures for *The Champion Pig* offers celebratory moments and rituals of everyday life like a first haircut, a wedding, girl scouts with their troupe flags, and a boy displaying his large catch of fish. The boy's proud grin and beaming face certainly are evidence of what he takes seriously. On the other hand, in a smiling portrait of Clark Gable (pl. 30) by Yousuf Karsh, the cultural aspects of what is being taken seriously are the admiration of our society for the good-looking, genial, sexy, macho man who is being photographed because he has become famous for having those attributes. There is

something in Gable's relaxed posture and amused face that suggests that he may not be taking himself as seriously as his culture does.

Norfleet supports her theories when she reproduces Joe Sternberg's pictures of suburban Floridians, for their patios, Tupperware parties and beach barbecues are certainly cultural indicators. However, the formal portrait or the snapshot close-up would seem to reveal more about individual personality than about the complexity of a culture.

That is, unless one is a deconstructionist philosopher who argues that we are all less individuals than composites of cultural indoctrinations: we not only view but also present ourselves according to our learned ideologies of personality. The needless – and often ludicrous – insistence on gender-identified clothes and hair-styles offers ample evidence that this learned behaviour is based on cultural demands. Carl Jung argued that individuals must recognize both the female and male aspects of their psyches before they can enjoy wholeness of being. The unisex revolutions of the 1960s reminded us of how threatening our society finds any suggestion that men and women share characteristics as part of their essential humanity. In judging photographic portraiture as an index to sexual identification as part of the "psychology" of an individual, therefore, we need to be aware of our own prejudices. Fortunately, the excessively rigid gender-identifications of past decades have been considerably relaxed.

To recapitulate: the interpretation of the psychology of an individual through a photographic portrait can be seen as being dependent on our answers to questions concerning theories of the universality of culture-specific expressions. Do psychological verities proclaim themselves in body postures, facial displays, or gestures? If so, has the photographer distorted these by psychological projections or æsthetic preconceptions? Can the photographer ever succeed in lifting the mask to reveal secrets of character? Is there only one "true self"? Does the camera artist have other preoccupations besides revelation of character – for example, reproduction problems for client publishers? Are we, the viewers of the portrait, incapacitated by prejudices? These are some of the fundamental issues.

Yousuf Karsh has been aware of many of these questions and has tried to answer them. In the case of the famous movie stars he photographed, he recognized the difficulty of separating the true personality of an actor from that of a favourite role. He knew also how much Hollywood stars are a part of our fantasy life. He acknowledged that he was more at home with certain personalities – musicians, especially, as well as painters and sculptors – than with others. What Karsh terms his quest, his search for greatness, has introduced viewers to some of the outstanding personalities of our time; he hopes that his pictures have given viewers an intimate glimpse of these individuals and greater insight into them than is ordinarily available. Given the complexities of psychological portraiture, I would have to say that Karsh's photographs reveal him as a supreme romantic, a perfectionist, a humanist par excellence, and, above all, an incurably good-humoured optimist. Anyone who says that "the heart and the mind are the true lens of the camera"[30] is also a creative artist with an ardent loyalty to the essence of great photography.

Notes

1. See the last chapter of Jeffrey Meyers, *Hemingway, a Biography* (New York: Harper and Row, 1986) for a detailed account of the accident and subsequent deterioration.

2. Quoted as the epigraph for Shirley Weitz, *Nonverbal Communication* (New York: Oxford University Press, 1974), n.p.

3. Weitz, p. 270.

4. John P. Spiegel and Paul Machotka, *Messages of the Body* (New York: The Free Press, [c. 1974]), p. 7.

5. Charles Darwin, *The Expression of the Emotions in Man and Animals* (New York: Appleton, 1873), p. 13.

6. Darwin, p. 13.

7. Darwin, p. 15.

8. Susan Sontag, *On Photography* (New York: Farrar, Straus and Giroux, 1977), p. 23.

9. Quoted in Sontag, p. 111.

10. Ben Maddow, "An Ironic Distance," *Exposure* XXV: 4 (Winter 1987), p. 9.

11. Yousuf Karsh, *Karsh Portfolio* (Toronto: University of Toronto Press, 1967), p. 10.

12. Mark L. Knapp, *Nonverbal Communication in Human Interaction*, 2nd ed. (New York: Holt, Rinehart and Winston, 1978), p. 178.

13. Anne Noggle, "Seeing Ourselves," in *Silver Lining: Photographs of Anne Noggle* (Albuquerque: University of New Mexico Press, 1983), p. 33.

14. Noggle, p. 32.

15. Quoted in Ben Maddow, *Faces: A Narrative History of the Portrait in Photography* (Boston: New York Graphic Society, 1977), p. 387.

16. Richard Avedon, Introduction to *In the American West* (New York: Harry N. Abrams, 1985), n.p.

17. Avedon, n.p.

18. Harold Rosenberg, "Portraits – A Meditation on Likeness," in *Richard Avedon Portraits*, 1st ed. (New York: McGraw-Hill, 1976), n.p.

19. Edward Hall, *The Silent Language* (New York: Doubleday, 1973) and *The Hidden Dimension* (New York: Doubleday, 1969).

20. Robert U. Akeret, *Photoanalysis*, (New York: Peter H. Wyden, 1973).

21. Max Kozloff, "Opaque Disclosures," *Art in America*, LXXV: 10 (October 1987), p. 147.

22. Quoted by Mark Haworth-Booth in his article "Bill Brandt: Behind the Camera," *Aperture*, 99 (Summer 1985), p. 40.

23. Haworth-Booth, p. 50.

24. Yousuf Karsh, *Karsh: A Fifty-Year Retrospective* (Toronto: University of Toronto Press, 1983), p. 23.

25. C. David Mortensen, *Basic Readings in Communication Theory*, 2nd ed. (New York: Harper and Row, 1979), p. 2.

26. Karsh, *A Fifty-Year Retrospective*, p. 150.

27. Casey Allen, "Philippe Halsman Interview," *Camera 35*, XXIII: 6 (July 1978), p. 70.

28. Alvin Langdon Coburn, *Men of Mark* (London: Duckworth and Company, 1913, and New York: M. Kennerley, 1913).

29. Barbara Norfleet, *The Champion Pig: Great Moments in Everyday Life* (Boston: David R. Godine, 1979), p. 3.

30. Karsh, *A Fifty-Year Retrospective*, p. 23.

The Portraitist at Work

Philip J. Pocock

There is a brief moment when all that there is in a man's mind and soul and spirit may be reflected through his eyes, his hands, his attitude. This is the moment to record. This is the elusive "moment of truth."

Yousuf Karsh, *In Search of Greatness*

Few attract international attention for the successful accomplishment of an ambitious long-term goal, one set in early adulthood. Fewer still, like Yousuf Karsh, garner international fame and fortune because of widespread public acceptance of the work required to achieve the goal.

As a young lad Yousuf Karsh wanted to become a surgeon, but in his early twenties, around 1930, he changed his focus. He did so while working in the photographic portrait studio of John H. Garo, in Boston. "There," Karsh writes, "I set my heart on photographing those men and women who leave their mark on the world."[1]

Years later, according to Helmut Gernsheim, the great collector of photographs, critic, and author, "our greatest representative of studio portraiture in the classical tradition is Yousuf Karsh of Ottawa."[2] In *The Picture History of Photography*, Peter Pollack concludes, "Karsh's great photographs . . . will impress future generations, who will know through his artistry the look of the celebrated persons of this period in history."[3]

Critics wishing to analyse Yousuf Karsh under a single rubric will fail to appreciate his real accomplishments, for there are so many "Karshes" from which to choose: the Armenian refugee; the immigrant; the apprentice; the Canadian (he possesses citizenship certificate number ten[4]); "Karsh of Ottawa"; the photographer; the entrepreneur; the conversationalist and raconteur; the religious believer; the artist; the collector; the portraitist; the photographic technician; the international exhibitor; the seeker of fame; the student of power; the respecter of greatness and devotee of the great . . . . But, taken singly, none of these one-dimensional "Karshes," fascinating though they may be, have alone determined his professional behaviour and his success. How can one assemble a complete picture from all these different images?

Karl Popper, the philosopher of science, suggests an approach. "The only intellectually important ends are: the formulations of problems; the tentative proposing of theories to solve them; and the critical discussion of the competing theories."[5] The methodology must be *problem-centred*.[6]

A pertinent application of Popper's insight is given by Bryan Magee, Senior Research Fellow in the History of Ideas at London University: "If one studies the work of, say, a philosopher, the first question one asks oneself is: 'What problem is he trying to solve?' In my experience most students of philosophy are not taught to ask, and do not think to ask themselves, this question. Rather they ask: 'What is he trying to say?' As a result they commonly have the experience of thinking they

113

understand what he is saying without seeing the point of his saying it. For only by understanding his problem-situation could they do that."[7]

In studying the work of Yousuf Karsh, therefore, the question to begin with is "what problem did he set out to solve?" Karsh himself suggests this is an appropriate starting point, for he writes: "I thrive on problems."[8]

A Focus on Power

In our approach to Karsh, we must consider the powerful insights and intentions provoked by the threatening problems within his early environment. Yousuf Karsh's first fifteen years were spent within the disintegrating and chaotic remnants of the once great and powerful Ottoman empire, an empire that had incorporated part of ancient Armenia. Karsh was born in Turkey, the formal remains of the Ottoman empire, on 23 December 1908, in Mardin, a town about twenty kilometres north of the border with Syria. It had a population of 27,000 on the eve of World War I, when Karsh was six years old.

Nagel's travel guide for Turkey describes Mardin as a place that was ruled at first by emirs subject to the Omeyyad – and then Abbassid – caliphs, and in 837 came under the rule of the Hamanid sovereigns. In the middle of the tenth century they were driven out by the Marwandis, who were in turn replaced by the Seljuks around 1080. From 1108, the Artukid Turks were the lords of Mardin, and they remained so for a long time despite the attacks by Saladin (1183), his son Melik Adil (1197–98), and his grandson Melik Ashraf (1202–03). In 1259–60, Mardin was besieged by the Mongols, to whom it surrendered after eight months of seige. In 1394, Tamerlane took the town and handed it to one of his brothers, Sultan Isa; after the latter's rebellion, Tamerlane reoccupied Mardin but was not able to take the citadel (1401).

After Isa's death, his brother, Salih, handed the town to the Turcoman ruler of the Kara Koyunlu (dynasty of the Black Sheep) in 1408; thirty years later the latter had to surrender it to the rival dynasty of the Ak Koyunlu (White Sheep). In 1507, the Sefevid Shah Ismail of Iran took the town and, according to a Venetian merchant, Mardin at that time contained more Christians and Jews than Muslims and had fine houses and mosques. In 1516, Selim I occupied the town. From 1832 to 1840, it was the scene of a Kurd revolt supported in 1839 by the Egyptian troops of Ibrahim Pasha.[9]

It is obvious that, for centuries, the lives of Mardin's citizens were determined by accident and force, not by free and peaceful reflection and choice. An Armenian priest explained to Karsh why he did not have the customary 'ian' at the end of his surname: ". . . to avoid drawing unnecessary attention to our race."[10] Karsh writes, "I had been brought up to speak Arabic, rather than Armenian, for the simple reason that in Mardin, Turkey, which was my home, when the Armenian language was spoken there were curses, and very often stones thrown in the street."[11] He recalls that, one day, he had returned from school with his forehead bleeding. "I had been stoned by Turkish boys who had tried to take away my only playthings, a few marbles."[12]

It is one thesis of this essay that the experiences and insights gained in Karsh's early days led to a preoccupation with power and problem-solving; with, on the one hand, power-holders who possess the ability to coerce and to marshal resources, and, on the other hand, people who suffer because their needs go unmet. He also admires those who, with no worldly power, benefit others by their power to entertain and enlighten. Therefore, is not the truly great person the one who utilizes the power at his or her command to solve or ease people's problems? Is it true that, without greatness, our hopes cannot be met? To both these questions Karsh has said "yes". His diligence "in search of greatness" (the title of his autobiography) is to confirm that our hopes are not in vain.

Mardin had always been an arena for deadly power-games, yet Karsh refers to it as "that rich Eden of ours," with "incomparable melons and other fruits."[13] Karsh writes that his memories of those days in Mardin "comprise a strange mixture of blood and beauty, of persecution and peace."[14] Two of his mother's brothers were arrested and killed, one suffocated, and the other thrown alive into a well to die. His mother's sister was also thrown into a well, but she was rescued. Karsh's young sister died in a typhus epidemic, and the epidemic was so severe that no burial service could be arranged.[15]

Regardless of the shortage of food, Karsh's mother took in a girl called Mary, "a young Armenian girl whom the Turks had turned loose, but not before they had torn both her eyes from their sockets."[16] Says Karsh, "It was the bitterest of ironies that Mardin, whose tiers of rising buildings were said to resemble the Hanging Gardens of Babylon, and whose succulent fruits convinced its inhabitants it was the original Garden of Eden, should have been the scene of the Turkish atrocities against the Armenians in 1915."[17]

Why were the Armenians (most of whom were Christian) so persecuted? Karsh writes: "Although Christians were a minority in my homeland, the Muslims depended on the Christians in commerce, industry, architecture (many of the mosques were built by Armenians) and indeed for almost anything that had to be done."[18] One of Karsh's murdered uncles, for example, was a calligrapher who produced illuminated manuscripts of passages from both the Bible and the Koran. Similarly, the Armenian father of the photographer John Garo was once invited to lecture on theological and philosophical topics to a group of Muslims outside of a Turkish mosque on a Friday morning – the holy day in Islam.[19]

However, by 1915 Turkey was at war with Britain, France, Italy, and Russia, and engaged on many fronts. The Turkish government regarded the Armenian population as a dangerous foreign element, despite pledges of loyalty – it had friends among the enemy who had launched an attack against the Dardanelles, and relatives in the Russian armies. Early in 1915, the Turkish government decided to deport the whole Armenian population of about 1.75 million to Syria and Mesopotamia. The *Encyclopædia Britannica* describes it as "a general deportation in which atrocities were committed on a large scale . . . . It is estimated that about 600,000 Armenians died or were massacred en route. About one-third escaped deportation."[20]

Karsh and his parents no longer wanted to stay in Turkey. He describes the day in 1922 when they heard that the Turkish government had given his family permission to emigrate. "There were hard conditions, of course, but my father was one of the first to accept them. We were to be allowed to dispose of personal effects such as clothing (we had, however, been robbed of most of our belongings) and we were then simply to leave the doors of our houses open and to depart. We were to undertake that we would never return to our homeland again. Nor have I done so.

"The Turkish government did not permit us to leave by an easy route. We could have reached the Syrian border quickly by train. Instead, we were obliged to travel by caravan, with the result that the sheik of every little Turkish village and hamlet was able to exact a further price from us for permission to proceed. It took us exactly twenty-nine days to complete the journey that would have taken less than two days by train. In the course of it, my parents were forced to part with every coin and valuable they had managed to set out with.

"The caravan was composed of Bedouins and Kurds carrying freight on donkeys and camels to

Fig. 31
Yousuf Karsh
Landscape 1926
Modern gelatin silver print from copy
negative
24.0 × 18.3 cm
National Archives of Canada, PA-165839

Aleppo in Syria. We were entirely at their mercy, and they had little of this virtue."[21]

Karsh was thirteen when the family, having lost all the resources garnered during a lifetime, set about to create a new home in Aleppo.

The early life of Yousuf Karsh is poignant, yet the horrors that he experienced are, unfortunately, not unique. Equally poignant are the tales from the fire bombings of London or Hamburg, the nuclear bombings of Hiroshima and Nagasaki, the madness of Auschwitz or the Katyn forest, the invasions of Vietnam or Afghanistan, the struggles of Belfast or Beirut. Karsh is noteworthy in that he used the horrors of his early experiences not as a source of bitterness, but rather to fuel his lifelong interest in the truly great, in those who have power and who wield it not for harm, but for good, not to exploit problems, but to solve them, not to submerge needs, but to answer them.

In 1924 Yousuf Karsh sailed from Beirut on the French liner *Versailles*, off to build a new life in the new world. He had his sixteenth birthday en route to Halifax, where he arrived on 31 December 1924, speaking Arabic and a little French, without money, and without having had a "real childhood."[22] He was met by his uncle George Nakash, his mother's brother.

The Apprenticeship Years

For a young penniless immigrant with very little formal education the first problem was: How do I earn a living? This difficult question was not answered through careful reflection and choice, but through force of circumstance combined with his great natural talents. Uncle Nakash was a portrait photographer in Sherbrooke, Quebec. Within months, formal schooling ceased and young Yousuf became absorbed by photography, which he mastered to the point where he won a photographic competition (fig. 31). Most enthralling were the human dimensions of photographic

116

portraiture. Karsh remembers working as an apprentice with his uncle in his studio. "I soon became acquainted with all the usual technical processes involved in developing, printing, and enlarging. But I particularly recall the special thrill I derived whenever Uncle Nakash had clients in for a sitting. It was then that I listened and watched most eagerly. I had to tune my ear to the special language of the studio, but the repartee between photographer and client always fascinated me."[23]

Uncle Nakash was pleased with young Yousuf's work, and arranged for him to be apprenticed to "one of the greatest photographers in the history of the art,"[24] John H. Garo of Boston (see fig. 2). There the twenty-year-old spent three years, from 1928 to 1931 (fig. 32). Garo sent him off to the Boston Public Library to study the reproductions of the work of the great portraitists, especially Rembrandt and Velasquez. "On a week-end," Karsh writes, "I would go to the Public Library . . . which had become my other home in Boston."[25]

Again, it was the human aspect of the art that fascinated him. Karsh writes that, when he went there in 1928, Garo's name was so famous in the world of photography that he had the sensation of being sent to study under a Michelangelo. "Garo's clientele was the aristocracy of Boston, and beyond. Although he did almost all his work in his studio, a practice that I have not followed, his portfolio was already filled with studies of nationally and internationally known personages, the great Americans of his day. He did not travel to find them either; they sought him out in Boston."[26]

In the late afternoons or evenings, there would often be spontaneous gatherings or parties in the elaborately decorated salon at Garo's studio. For example, there was a Hallowe'en party of seventy friends in the reception salon, "and many other parties where there was entertainment of extraordinary talent, displayed wholly for its own

Fig. 32
John H. Garo (American, 1870–1939)
Yousuf Karsh 1929
Gelatin silver, printed later
25.3 × 19.0 cm
Collection of the artist

enjoyment," as well as "many a happy and relaxed gathering of artists in a host of fields."[27] At other times, the gatherings would be planned in advance, and would include visiting artists of the theatre or opera who could be expected in Boston at such a time. Karsh recalls that sometimes they would hear a great star sing *The Song of the Flea*, or an aria from *Boris Godounoff*, with parts filled in by others present until the whole assembly shared in the chorus, including himself. "An air of cultured informality surrounded Garo and all his interests," he writes, and adds that he was able to share in wonderful conversations and study some of the great personalities in the world of music, letters, the theatre, and the opera of the nineteen-twenties. "It was an opportunity for me to listen to wise men and brilliant women conversing. Those were glorious afternoons and evenings, and I knew them to be so even at the time. Garo's salon was my university, a noble institution at which to have been permitted to study."[28]

But Karsh learned most by closely observing, questioning, and judging everything that Garo did. This critical stance was encouraged by Garo. "He did not want me to see the same things as he saw," Karsh writes, "as long as I understood what I saw, as long as I saw clearly. . . . Always Garo encouraged independent thinking . . . it was his inspiration rather than his technique that would be the richest gift he could bestow on me."[29]

About twenty years ago, Beaumont Newhall told me that the key to understanding Yousuf Karsh was John Garo. Karsh learned from the weaknesses, as well as the strengths, of Garo's professional career. "One of Garo's great gifts," Karsh writes, "was his ability to fascinate, to enchant the subject to such an extent that the latter was really unaware of the act of photographing."[30] Garo used charm to relax his sitters. "When immersed in his work, he could suddenly exclaim to a tense subject, 'Now let me sing you an aria from *Aïda*!' And sing it he would in his fine bass-baritone." But

Karsh points to a deficiency: "He would project his personality in the studio, while hiding it in public." Although he looked like Mark Twain he did not have "his flair for publicity, or for the epigram." Garo was "modest all the way into his soul"; he lacked ambition. "This reticence," Karsh concludes, "no doubt kept Garo from much of the fame that could have been his. It kept him apart from the public, but he did not seem to care. He made portraits that were classics, but he did not even give them the momentum they could have received from one another in a collective showing. Therefore they are not remembered as a portfolio . . . there was no Garo collection known to the world, for the simple reason that none existed anywhere."[31]

Unlike Garo, at the very beginning of his career Karsh knew it was fame that he sought. "I know that it is not money you want," Solange Gauthier said to Karsh during the early days of their acquaintance in Ottawa (later she became Karsh's wife); she had asked him what he wanted out of life. "I agreed that it was not money," Karsh writes, "but went on, innocently enough, to say that I would like fame – some day I would rather like to be famous!"[32] But, as Karsh's subsequent behaviour has proven, it was not notoriety that he sought. Rather, it was fame gained by earning recognition and respect for one's expertise and artistry that was Karsh's lifelong goal. To do this, he would use his obsession with the powerful and great of mind, action, and spirit, an obsession nurtured in Garo's studio, to bring him a deserved and hard-earned personal stature.

In addition, thought Karsh, Garo was imprudent: he allowed himself to be exploited by his friends; he did not amass sufficient wealth to avoid poverty in later life. According to Karsh, Garo attracted friends, but perhaps this was because they found his studio an outlet through which they could express themselves; Garo himself may not have been so close to their hearts. Karsh

118

writes that Garo enjoyed his friends most when he could persuade them to impose upon him, "and impose upon him they did in the end. They came to his studio, they enjoyed his hospitality. With the stock market crash they came and borrowed his money . . . . Doubtless he suffered financial losses as the result of his own stock speculations (I have never bought a penny's worth of stock), but I fear that his speculations on some of his friends must have brought his bitterest setbacks."[33]

Karsh worked under Garo towards the end of the master's career (Garo died on 1 October 1939), and so was able to plan his professional life as he carefully and critically evaluated Garo's successes and failures. By the time he returned to Canada in 1931, twenty-three-year-old Yousuf Karsh had decided how he would solve the problem of earning a living.

It was understandable that Garo continued using the technology he knew best. But the younger man, to prepare for the future, would have to assess the opportunities afforded by the improvements in film and artificial lighting equipment. Because Garo used slower emulsions than were available at that time, he depended on brief time exposures rather than instantaneous shutter openings. This reduced portrait options. In addition, Garo did not use artificial light, which meant he could not photograph clients after about four o'clock in the afternoon.

This was contrary to the practice of the most celebrated portrait photographer of the day, Edward J. Steichen. Like Karsh much later with his photograph of Winston Churchill, Steichen had also become widely known as a young man for a portrait – in his case, of J. Pierpont Morgan (fig. 33).

When Edward Steichen went to New York in 1923, at age forty-four, he bought a copy of *Vanity Fair* magazine and found his picture in it along with the caption: "The greatest living portrait photographer." Steichen contacted the editor,

Fig. 33
Edward Steichen (American, 1879–1973)
J. Pierpont Morgan 1903
Photogravure
20.6 × 15.5 cm
National Gallery of Canada, 34999.67
Gift of Dorothy Meigs Eidlitz, St. Andrews, New Brunswick
From *Camera Work: Steichen Supplement* (April 1906)

Frank Crowninshield, and negotiated a job as chief photographer for *Vanity Fair*, for which he would take portraits of celebrities, many of them from the performing arts; he also contracted to make fashion photographs for *Vogue*. To date he had never used artificial light in portraiture, but it was forced upon him by the magazine's electrician when he went to make his first fashion photograph. "After that experience," Steichen writes, "I realized that electric light would be my greatest ally in getting variety . . . gradually I added lights, one at a time, until, in later years of my work for *Vogue* and *Vanity Fair*, there were lights going all over the place."[34]

When Karsh went to Boston in 1928, Steichen was the best known magazine-sponsored portrait photographer of the time, and in his masterful work the young Karsh would have seen the benefits of artificial light, benefits which he would make use of in future years.

Just before Karsh arrived, for example, there was a dramatic stage-lit portrait of Fred Astaire, with the smoke plume from his lighted cigarette caught by the new lighting techniques. The cigarette, often with its smoke plume fixed by flash, is found in many Karsh portraits (fig. 34).

In 1928, there was a portrait of Jascha Heifetz playing his violin, with a huge shadow replica on the wall. In a similar vein, Steichen took a self-portrait surrounded by photographic apparatus, again with shadows looming on the wall behind. Maurice Chevalier doing a song-and-dance – accompanied by huge double shadows – was published in 1929.

The year Karsh returned to Canada, 1931, saw Steichen's pictures of Katharine Cornell, Martha Graham, Charlie Chaplin, H.G. Wells, and many more. In addition, *Vogue* was publishing Steichen's innovative fashion photographs, and he was doing advertising photographs for the J. Walter Thompson agency, an agency that, years later, gave commissions to Karsh. On his way back to Canada,

the younger man visited the elder; Karsh says that they talked for about "three cigarettes' worth of time."[35]

The Steichen photographs of celebrities continued. In 1932, the year in which Karsh opened his Ottawa studio using the corporate name "Karsh of Ottawa," among those that *Vogue* published were Steichen's portraits of Noël Coward, Dorothy Parker, W.B. Yeats, and Winston Churchill. Although Karsh was in Canada, these portraits were very much on his mind, for during this period he twice borrowed a scrapbook of Steichen's magazine photographs from a fellow Canadian photographer who was equally enchanted by them.[36]

In 1944 Karsh photographed Steichen. Karsh writes that "Steichen pioneered in establishing photography as an art. He brought to every branch of photography his inventive genius. I was commissioned to photograph him during the Second World War, when he was a Naval Commander. The prospect of photographing such a giant was awesome. I was so tense and nervous that the first unsatisfactory result made me timorously request a second sitting, to which a patient and understanding Steichen acquiesced. Years later we were to laugh about this, when my wife Estrellita and I were guests of Steichen and his wife Joanna at their Ridgefield, Connecticut, home in the 1960s . . . . In his later years [c. 1965] Steichen resembled an Old Testament patriarch."[37]

Steichen comments that, "For *Vanity Fair* began a long procession of portraits of the great, the near-great, and the would-be-great. It didn't matter whether the sitter was a statesman, a writer, a poet, an actor, a prizefighter, or a musician; they were all interesting. The exciting thing was the variety in this procession that came to my studio."[38] Like Karsh in later years, Steichen was involved with "greatness." But, like Garo, he had no desire to put together a large and significant collection of portraits, and therefore did not leave his studio to hunt for the great. They were simply directed to him by his editor. "Karsh of Ottawa" would do it differently.

The Photographer at Work

Economic necessity forced Karsh to be very clear regarding the difference between the professional photographer and the amateur photographer. "Every day we witness commendable amateur efforts," Karsh writes, "I mean amateur in the true sense, that is, taken by *people who do not earn their living through photography*. We must always be prepared for happy surprises from such amateurs, because they are the most likely of all to be uninhibited in their approach."[39] [Emphasis added.]

A few amateurs have made significant contributions to the world's stock of photographs. The British photographer Julia Margaret Cameron (1815–79) took up the hobby in middle age. She entertained many of the celebrities of her day: Tennyson, Carlyle, Darwin, Browning, Longfellow. "Her dynamic portraits," Beaumont Newhall writes, "are among the most noble and impressive yet produced by means of the camera,"[40] (see fig. 8). In another example, Charles Lutwidge Dodgson, lecturer on mathematics at Oxford, better known as Lewis Carroll (1832–98) and the author of the *Alice* books, has been described as "the best photographer of children in the nineteenth century."[41]

Many writers have been active amateur photographers, and I myself have had the pleasure of discovering the Irish photographs of J.M. Synge.[42] A few remarkable photographers have come from wealthy families, amateurs unfettered by financial need.

By contrast, some who have earned their livings by supplying photographs to clients have become world famous, not for their professional work, but

Fig. 34
Yousuf Karsh
Thornton Wilder 24 May 1956
Gelatin silver, printed later
49.7 × 39.1 cm
National Archives of Canada, PA-165848

for the photographs they have made in their spare time. Paul Caponigro, Elliott Erwitt, André Kertész are among those photographers who have made their livings by taking commercial photographs of which the public are not aware, but who have earned honoured places in the pantheon of photography for making photographs unrelated to income or client demands. The motives are many: to explore new possibilities of photographic technology, to express the self, to explore and record the external world.

Portrait photography has also been a favoured profession for those who love the photographic process and who need to earn a living. Karsh writes about his early years that "everything connected with the art of photography captivated my interest and energy – it was to be not only my livelihood, but my continuing passion."[43]

Sometimes an amateur turns to this hobby in order to earn income. For example, during the nineteenth century, when everyone rushed to have a portrait made by the new daguerreotype process, Anton Martin, earlier an assistant in physics at the Polytechnic Institute, Vienna, earned his income in the newly created trade as an itinerant portraitist in Germany.[44]

There is also a case of a banker turning his photographic hobby into a profession – Emil Otto Hoppé, the son of a German banking family, who, after twelve years, left his London bank in 1907 to become a portrait photographer. Already he was a prominent exhibitor and influential writer on photography in English and foreign journals; he was a founder of the London Salon (in which Karsh has exhibited.)

Hoppé advocated a natural approach to portraiture, one that avoided the contrived style popular at the time. For eighteen years he entertained and took portraits of celebrities in his studio, which had previously been that of John Millais. He published many collections of portraits of "men of mark." Subsequently he spent twenty years tour-ing the world, taking photographs for the *Orbis Terrarum* series of topographical books. Born in 1878, he was still exhibiting in 1954. Up until World War II his books were well known in England and Germany. However there is little written about him under the rubric of "photography," for professional success using photographic means does not always gain acclaim from the various academies dedicated to honouring photography.[45]

The most remarkable intrusion of amateurs into the world of photography was that of two distinguished professional musicians, Leopold D. Mannes and Leo Godowsky, Jr., who developed the idea for Kodachrome colour film.[46] Very often it is the *outsider*, and not the professional insider, who makes the most successful inventions and innovations; and this holds for many other things: among them, the jet engine, xerography, the transistor, and the personal computer.

Even Karsh's famous contemporary, Henri Cartier-Bresson (they were both born in 1908), was in a sense an amateur. Unlike Karsh, he did not have the problem of economic survival. Cartier-Bresson went to Marseilles in 1932, at age twenty-four. "A small allowance enabled me to get along, and I worked with enjoyment," he writes. "I had just discovered the Leica [the first 35 mm camera]. It became the extension of my eye, and I have never been separated from it since I found it. I prowled the streets all day, feeling very strung-up and ready to pounce, *determined to 'trap' life – to preserve life in the act of living*. Above all, I craved to seize the whole essence, in the confines of one single photograph, of some situation that was in the process of unrolling itself before my eyes . . . . To me, photography is the simultaneous recognition, in a fraction of a second, of the significance of an event as well as of a precise organization of forms which give that event its proper expression. I believe that, through the act of living, the discovery of oneself is made

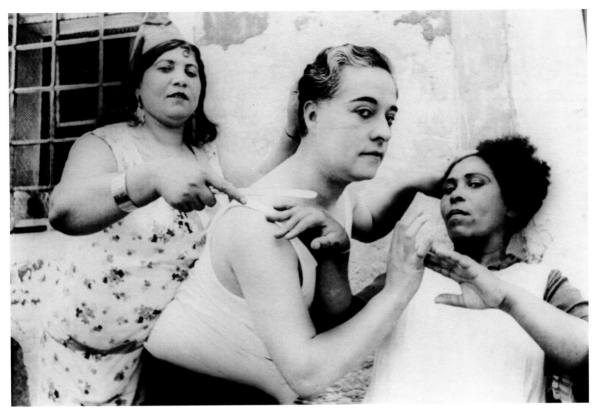

Fig. 35
Henri Cartier-Bresson (French, b. 1908)
Alicante, Spain 1933
Gelatin silver, printed prior to 1947
16.5 × 29.4 cm
National Gallery of Canada, 28588

concurrently with the discovery of the world round us which can mold us, but which can also be affected by us. A balance must be established between these two worlds – the one inside us and the one outside us."[47] [Emphasis added.]

In Cartier-Bresson's statement there is no hint of the need to earn a living by means of the camera; total attention could be directed to the æsthetics and the intellectual rationale of photography – a very different situation from that of Yousuf Karsh.

In contrast, the young Frenchman had been blessed by educational experiences made possible by family wealth, within the confines of peaceful Europe. At twenty, after deciding against entering the family business, Cartier-Bresson began two years of study under the painter André Lhote, after

123

which he spent eight months in Cambridge, England, painting and attending literature classes.[48] By 1929, he had become interested in the photographs of Man Ray and Eugène Atget. In 1931 he moved to Africa and lived in a village on the French Ivory Coast, where he took pictures with a small roll-film camera. As a result, Cartier-Bresson's health became weakened by black-water fever, which in turn required some time of tranquil travel for recuperation. Such personal and economic expenses were not ones which the young Karsh could have absorbed. Furthermore, money the young immigrant obtained was used to help his family in Aleppo, Syria.

Cartier-Bresson's relative economic freedom allowed him to develop his photographic approach unhampered by tradition, or by the immediate demands of clients. In fact, Cartier-Bresson rejected commercial portraiture. "It seems to me it would be pretty difficult to be a portrait photographer for customers who order and pay since, apart from a Mæcenas or two, they want to be flattered, and the result is no longer real . . . . The sitter is suspicious of the objectivity of the camera, while what the photographer is after is an acute psychological study of the sitter."[49]

In discussing portrait painters, Max J. Friedlander distinguishes "more or less fruitfully" between "portraitists who make use of the medium of painting, and painters who make portraits. Frans Hals belongs to the first group, Titian to the second."[50]

Similarly, there are portraitists who make use of the medium of photography, and photographers who make portraits. With regard to the work by which he is known, Yousuf Karsh belongs to the first group; Henri Cartier-Bresson belongs to the second.

In the first category the intention is closely defined: making a photographic portrait. In the second category the object is the creation of what is chemically and physically a photograph, but the photographer is restricted only by intentionality, æsthetic vision, and practical abilities. The intention may be undeclared, even obscure – sometimes the intention may be to make a portrait, but if the focus is on *photography* and not portraiture, there will probably exist the intention to achieve a new æsthetic vision, an untraditional approach, or an innovative use of photographic technology.

It was to convalesce that Cartier-Bresson went to Marseilles in 1932, and during the year following he managed to travel through Middle Europe (fig. 35) and Italy. In 1935 he went to Mexico, and then was off to the United States in 1936 where, at age twenty-eight, he exhibited with Walker Evans at the Julien Levy Gallery. He had spent four years developing his own unique photographic approach, which was to be as inconspicuous as possible. He writes: "Approach tenderly, gently. . . on tiptoe – even if the subject is still life. A velvet hand, a hawk's eye – these we should all have. It's no good jostling or elbowing. And no photographs taken with the aid of flashlight either, if only out of respect for the actual light – even when there isn't any of it."[51]

Karsh, with his need both to build up his international portfolio of portraits and to please his subjects and clients, had less room for unfettered experimentation. At times his sitters allowed him no leisure – he had to rush if he was to fulfil his commission. He could not afford the luxury of remaining inconspicuous for long periods, and instead used his innovative powers to obtain the opportunities for making portraits; his considerable charm was used to help his subjects to relax and let their less public faces through. His mastery of artificial light allowed him to maximize his use of time.

Similar considerations affected their differing approaches to travel. In 1932, when Cartier-Bresson was setting out to explore the use of his small camera as a tool to capture life, the equally

124

125

Fig. 36
Yousuf Karsh
Saint John, New Brunswick 1952
Gelatin silver, printed 1989
40.0 × 39.3 cm
Collection of the artist
For the *Maclean's* assignment "Face of Canada"

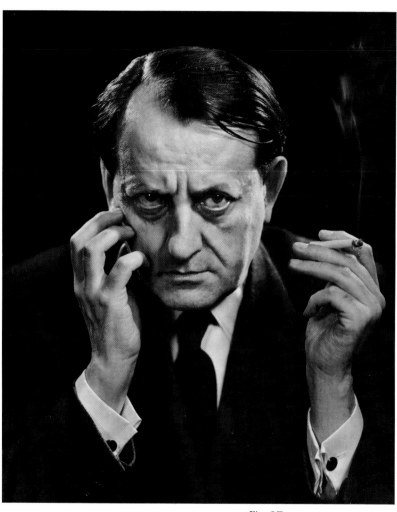

Fig. 37
Yousuf Karsh
André Malraux 3 June 1954
Gelatin silver, printed 1988
49.9 × 40.2 cm
National Gallery of Canada
Gift of the artist

young Yousuf Karsh moved to Ottawa and, with no financial resources, set up as a portrait photographer. In the early years, he travelled most often when on assignment.

"I have travelled a good deal," Cartier-Bresson writes, "I like to take my time about it, leaving between one country and the next an interval in which to digest what I've seen. Once I have arrived in a new country, I feel almost like settling down there, so as to live on proper terms with the country. I could never be a globe trotter."[52] About the time when Cartier-Bresson wrote the above, 1952, *Maclean's* magazine assigned Yousuf Karsh to photograph Canadian cities, including among others Saint John (fig. 36), Quebec City (pl. 38), Montreal (pl. 20), Ottawa (see fig. 14), and Vancouver (see fig. 51).

By 1952, Karsh and Cartier-Bresson were approaching their mid-forties; they seemed well launched into predictable careers. In that year Cartier-Bresson wrote: "I regard myself still as an amateur, though I am no longer a dilettante."[53] In 1946 Cartier-Bresson had had a solo show at New York's Museum of Modern Art, and 1952 was the year of publication of his first major book, *The Decisive Moment*. Karsh had already published his first big book, *Faces of Destiny* (1946).

In the next few years, Cartier-Bresson, who had pioneered a particular use of the 35 mm camera and had impressed an æsthetic of vision and mode of behaviour on many young photographers, continued travelling widely, collecting photographs that would result in other major publications, in quick succession: *From One China to Another* (1954); *Les Dances à Bali* (1954); *The Europeans* (1955); *People of Moscow* (1955). In 1957 a large Cartier-Bresson retrospective exhibition, initiated at Pavillon de Marsan, at the Louvre, Paris, would travel throughout Europe, Japan, and the United States. By the late fifties Cartier-Bresson had achieved fame within the photographic community.

In the fifties, Karsh strengthened his international portfolio by travelling extensively in Europe and North America to hunt down and photograph people of great talent or responsibility. Among the new subjects were: Albert Camus, Pablo Casals (pl. 36), René Clair, Paul Claudel (see fig. 43), Alfred Cortot.... It was as if Karsh was working alphabetically through the list of world celebrities (fig. 37), working towards the publication of *Portraits of Greatness* in 1959, and the preparation of a major exhibition of his prints, *Portraits of Greatness*, which opened at the National Gallery of Canada in 1960; the exhibition also toured Canada. He engaged as well in some non-portrait photography. For example, *Time* commissioned him to go to the Arctic and photograph wild flowers in colour.[54]

The parallel careers of Henri Cartier-Bresson and Yousuf Karsh are illustrative of the different ways in which the camera may be used to earn recognition and fame. Both were born in 1908, both began camera-based careers around 1930, and today both are household names; there the similarity stops. Cartier-Bresson was able to travel and explore the use of the Leica 35 mm camera as a young man with an allowance; he rejected the large-format camera and the traditional approach to photographic portraiture. Karsh, a penniless immigrant to Canada, began his professional career as a traditional portrait photographer, using a large-format camera. Cartier-Bresson embraced available light in which to photograph; Karsh mastered the use of artificial light. Cartier-Bresson became known for his "decisive moment"; Karsh became known for his "search for greatness."

The different personalities of the two men, arising from very different historical and cultural situations, led inevitably to their differing styles: Cartier-Bresson's fascination with the vivid, passing moment, the anonymous subject, the experimental limits of photography; and Karsh's focus on the carefully posed, compassionately and classi-cally presented well-known artist or leader. The boundaries of their explorations were set from the beginning by the different problems they each faced.

"You should make Karsh your President – or whatever you have in Canada," W. Eugene Smith said to me, "He can do anything. He can even walk through walls!"[55] The particular abilities which enabled Karsh to solve his professional problems with such success are demonstrated in another aspect by comparison with this talented and courageous photojournalist.

Smith had just been taken by Karsh, whom he had met only hours before, on a tour of Montreal's Expo 67. To Smith's surprise, Karsh carried no press or V.I.P. pass to ensure easy access to Expo's many pavilions. Nevertheless, he took Smith to the head of the long line of people who had waited for hours for entrance to the U.S. pavilion, and within very few minutes of Karsh's brief conversation with the Marine guarding the door, Smith and Karsh were being greeted warmly by the commissioner general. Soon they were comfortably seated in the pavilion's air-conditioned V.I.P. lounge. The guides, after serving refreshments, took them on a tour. What had Karsh said to the guard? Smith's account went something like this: "Young man, it gives me great pleasure to introduce to you one of America's true heroes, Eugene Smith, an honoured war photographer whose work has won world acclaim." After the rituals of introduction were performed, Karsh added: "I am sure that your commissioner general would find it a great honour for Gene Smith to visit your most distinguished pavilion." That, according to Smith, was all that it took.

What Smith had witnessed was the fact that Karsh has charm in the sense defined by Albert Camus: "You know what charm is: a way of getting the answer yes without having asked any clear question."[56] Without an appreciation of Karsh's charm, grace, and interpersonal skills, it is impossible to fully understand the success of his professional career.

Smith developed a strong liking for Karsh, as do others involved with photography who have not only met him but who have been able to engage in a lively interaction with him: Edward Steichen, for example.[57] Smith had found more than "Karsh of Ottawa," the camera-portraitist who runs ads in *The New Yorker* magazine;[58] the man who had taken away Churchill's cigar. He had found a multi-talented, energetic and effective personality, and enjoyed discovering how much fun it was to be with him.

But this meeting demonstrated something more than Karsh's ability to charm and entertain (fig. 38). In the 1960s Eugene Smith and Yousuf Karsh would appear as occupying antipodean positions in the world of professional photography. By then, both were famous in the popular media. For example, the *Encyclopædia Britannica* had declared that Smith was a "photojournalist whose compassionate and psychologically penetrating photoessays made him one of the most important photographers of the mid-20th century,"[59] and that Karsh was a "photographer whose outstanding portraits of the great men of his time are characterized by psychological insight and flawless technique."[60] Both were great successes, yet they appeared to be from hostile camps.

Smith always chose to be a participant as well as an observer, and during World War II he insisted on sharing the risks of infantrymen while on assignment in the Pacific and was severely wounded by shrapnel. Karsh took the risk of crossing the submarine-infested North Atlantic in 1943 on a freighter carrying explosives, but he photographed the people at the top, not in the trenches. It is claimed, however, that Karsh's wartime portrait of Winston Churchill was an "icon" for the British people. One writer states that the well-known image "became a symbol of

Fig. 38
Yousuf Karsh on Assignment June–July 1958
Gelatin silver print
24.1 × 19.3 cm
National Archives of Canada, PA-165850
Photo: A.V. Roe (Canada), Malton, Ontario

128

England's will to fight. The strength and power of Churchill's face stiffened the resolution of the English people.... The people loved the photograph; it was easy to imagine Churchill's stirring speeches issuing from this indomitable face."[61] Helmut Gernsheim wrote in 1962 that Karsh's famous wartime portrait "will, I am convinced, outlive all other representations of the great man in any medium, for the simple reason that it is more characteristic of him than any other portrait I know. And I should know, for no fewer than 80,000 portraits of Churchill passed through my hands when I was compiling my pictorial biography of him."[62]

Another apparent difference between Karsh and Smith was their relation to industry and the media. Smith was a hero to the radical young photographers in the 1960s. He was seen as not having "sold out to the establishment."[63] John Szarkowski, Director of the Department of Photography of the Museum of Modern Art, New York, claims that W. Eugene Smith came to be regarded as a patron saint among magazine photographers, not only because of the excellence of his work, but because he quit *Life* magazine in protest not once but twice, in 1941 and in 1954.[64]

Szarkowski explains: "Gene Smith was perhaps the photographer who tried most heroically to make the magazine photostory meet the standards of coherence, intensity, and personal accountability that one expects of a work of art. Predictably, his insistence on personal accountability did not fit comfortably into the system of group journalism."[65]

By contrast, Yousuf Karsh was not making photostories but rather portraits of people whose position often made them newsworthy. He worked comfortably with *Life* magazine, as did many others, such as the portrait photographer Philippe Halsman. In 1944 Karsh writes that he was "in Washington carrying out a marvellous assignment given me by *Life* to portray some seventy-odd dignitaries [including J. Edgar Hoover and John L. Lewis (pl. 8)] who were then gathered in the nation's capital."[66] In 1945 *Life* commissioned Karsh to photograph delegates to the San Francisco Conference which founded the United Nations Organization; he photographed Dean Acheson, King Faisal of Saudi Arabia, and V.M. Molotov. In the winter of 1945–46 *Life* commissioned him to do a portfolio: "Portraits of Captains of Industry."[67] In January of 1946 *Life* sent Karsh to Hollywood, where he photographed twenty stars; he comments: "It was . . . an interesting experience, since I find actors very challenging subjects, if only because of the difficulty of reaching their natural personalities."[68] Karsh had a continuing professional relationship with *Life*.

Most young photographers after World War II, especially those in the West, considered that the illustrated magazines of North America and Europe such as *Life, Picture Post, Paris Match, Stern*, and *Epoca* would provide *the* market for their photographs. Indeed, for about two decades, these periodicals provided a huge source of revenue for photographers. It was this rich and growing market that led Cartier-Bresson, along with a few of his friends, to form, in New York in the spring of 1947, the photo agency *Magnum*. When Yousuf Karsh was at his prime, the illustrated magazines were at their circulation peak, and Karsh portraits were much sought after, for people always want to see those who affect their world.

Commissions from other sources included, for example, the J. Walter Thompson advertising agency commission to do portraits of twenty-seven musicians for RCA Victor in 1945 and 1946; the portraits were used for publicity and record jackets.

This was a very different world of photography than that inhabited by Gene Smith. Smith's famous photoessay on Pittsburgh was not shot in the board room of a steel company; it was a view from the factory-blackened streets.[69]

129

Similarly, Smith went to Minimata, Japan, not to photograph executives, but to fight against the dangerous mercury pollution caused by the Chisso Corporation. He ended up being badly beaten for his efforts, but his work helped bring corrective measures.[70]

Nevertheless, the many accidental differences between the ways in which Karsh and Smith used photography are superficial compared with the similarity of their talents for gaining individual success. Within their own circumstances, and each in their own manner, they shared what can only be called the *ability to become famous*. For each, their fame rests not on doing things *for* photography, but in doing important things *with* photography.

Portraits of the Powerful

Yousuf Karsh is the most widely known and publicly acclaimed portraitist of our times, in any medium. Properly he is called a portraitist and not a photographer, for he defines himself thus: "Portrait photography is my chosen profession and I love it." He wrote this in his early fifties, adding: "And I hope that as I work along I will learn something new every day."[71]

Yousuf Karsh's driving force is his insatiable curiosity about people of power. The power to rule, to change, to create, to entertain, to enlighten, to win. Haunting him since his formative days in the troubled Middle East has been the problem and paradox of power: power, as Napoleon said, is uncreative, yet human needs can not be assuaged without exercising it.

But Karsh is wary of those who have only the power to get ahead; of those who fit G.K. Chesterton's description: "He had a great amount of intellectual capacity, of that peculiar kind which raises a man from throne to throne and lets him die loaded with honours without having either amused or enlightened the mind of a single man."[72] Karsh also knows that "half the experts are below average,"[73] and he tries always to seek out the best as subjects or colleagues.

These two strains – the obsessive curiosity about power, and about people – come together in portraiture and in the central question, directly addressed by Karsh, of how to capture the essence of a person in a single image. "I am a photographer and not a writer," Karsh writes, "my camera is, I trust, more powerful than my pen."[74] Yet Karsh has clearly articulated many of his views. He writes: "The aim and the art of the portraitist who works with a camera are not merely to produce a likeness but to reveal the mind and the soul behind the human face."[75] This is similar to the view expressed by Leonardo da Vinci that "you shall paint faces in such a way that it will be easy to understand what is going on in the mind, otherwise your art is unworthy of praise"; a view summarized by Jean Alazard as "a portrait should reveal the mind or soul of the model."[76] Karsh has frequently espoused this classical view of portraiture. From this perspective, Karsh writes about a portrait of Jean Sibelius (pl. 10) that his "courteous and charming manners never concealed his tremendous, vibrating soul, the power and emotional depth of his spirit, or the commanding aura of genius that surrounded him . . . . I was able to secure a whole series of portraits, but the one that is my favourite shows the composer with his eyes almost closed, listening to an upward surge of music in his imagination . . . . For me at least, the strong and sombre strains of 'Finlandia' resound from the portrait."[77]

These are not the words of someone straining to bend photographic technique to produce new or startling images. They are the sentiments of a self-declared "hero worshipper"[78] in a relentless search to add portraits to his "collection."[79] It is difficult to imagine Karsh prowling the streets with a miniature camera, alone and on tiptoe like Cartier-Bresson, because of, first, Karsh's need for

130

constant and challenging human interaction, and, second, his wish to photograph people whose power he acknowledges and respects.

He confirmed this approach with regard to a series of non-portrait illustrated books with which he was involved from 1958 to 1961. Karsh is a man of faith. He writes, "Although I was brought up and remain today a member of the Roman Catholic faith, I cannot aspire ever to become more than one of its lesser saints."[80] In 1952 Karsh had photographed Bishop Fulton J. Sheen, the charismatic television performer, and in 1957 a publisher asked Karsh to work with Sheen to make an English-language edition of *This Is the Mass* (the original text was by the well-known French Catholic historian Henri Daniel-Rops).[81] Karsh accepted. He was impressed by Sheen's skills and

Fig. 39
David Hume Kennerly (American, b. 1947)
Yousuf Karsh with President Gerald Ford and Betty Ford 6 June 1977
Gelatin silver print
15.6 × 23.7 cm
National Archives of Canada, PA-165849

their collaboration produced other books: *This Is Rome, A Pilgrimage in Words and Pictures*, conducted by Fulton J. Sheen, photographed by Yousuf Karsh and described by H. V. Morton (1960); and *These Are the Sacraments* (1962). In all of this Karsh was able to use his photographic skills in collaboration with people for whose talents he had great regard.

He writes: "The photographs that have given me the greatest satisfaction are, with a few notable exceptions, those of *people of consequence* . . . . They have included scientists, labour leaders, captains of industry, physicians, film stars, directors, composers, statesmen, clergymen, military leaders, princes, and presidents . . . . I seriously doubt if the interpretation of an unknown face is likely to have interest equal to that of a known personality, either to a photographer or to those who view his work. The best proof of this is that my portraits of famous people are better known than any of my other photographs."[82]

Karsh has described himself as "the photographer of personalities"[83] and "the photographer of popes and presidents and kings" (fig. 39).[84] He titled his first collection of portraits, published in 1946, *Faces of Destiny*,[85] and his lovingly published 1959 collection *Portraits of Greatness*. Altogether he has met his goal of building a sizeable international collection of portraits of people acclaimed because of their position, creative talent, authority or power. At the time of Karsh's eightieth birthday, John F. Burns, of *The New York Times*, was able to write, "his 50,000 portraits have become an honor role of the most distinguished Westerners of his time."[86]

Yet he regretted not having photographed two notable power-holders for his collection. "My heart's desire," Karsh wrote in 1945, "is to photograph Stalin, coupled with my great regret at never having secured the opportunity that I desired to make a portrait of Roosevelt so as to include these two great world leaders in my collection of portraits, to keep company with my Churchill."[87]

In Karsh's vocabulary "great" is often a word behind which lurks the primal attraction of power. Karsh's description of photographing Thomas Mann is suggestive. He begins his comments by noting that "many critics would say, and doubtless with good reason, that the late Thomas Mann was the greatest literary figure of his time," and he concludes, "Mann, I think, would have made an excellent subject for Dürer, who admired men of power."[88] Mann knew the polarity between greatness and power. Goethe, Karsh tells us, was Mann's idol, and in his novel *Lotte in Weimar* Mann has the sixty-eight-year-old Goethe say: "The fools don't know a great poet is first of all great and after that a poet. Don't you see it's all the same whether a man writes poetry or fights battles . . . . And greatness only comes with age. A young man can be a genius, but he cannot be great. Greatness comes only with the weight, endurance, power, mental equipment of age. Mind and power are products of age, they are what make up greatness."[89]

Mann also understood the polarity between greatness and goodness; in an essay on Heinrich Heine he wrote: "Heinrich Heine was not a 'good' man. He was only a great man."[90] Here Mann touched upon the trinity that has captivated Karsh's curiosity: the powerful, the great, and the good.

Karsh does not automatically attribute "greatness" to politicians. In the introduction to *Portraits of Greatness* he warns that, "when I came to assemble from my collection the portraits which I wished to include in this book, I discovered that it was greatness and humanity as exhibited in certain kinds of people to which I have responded with most warmth and excitement . . . it does not include politicians as such – Mr. Eisenhower appears as a leader of men in war, Mr. Pearson as a leader of men seeking peace."[91]

Fig. 40
Yousuf Karsh
Albert Einstein 11 February 1948
Gelatin silver print
27.8 × 32.9 cm
National Archives of Canada, PA-165943

Another politician, Konrad Adenauer (pl. 40),
also appeared in this Karsh collection, and Karsh
comments that "the German whom Churchill has
called the greatest of his race since Bismarck . . .
had become the master of his people; he had
brought them back to the family of Western
nations."[92] In Karsh's view, a politician does not
become great simply by being elected; he or she
must solve problems, not exploit them.

Karsh finds that photographing politicians presents unique problems. He gives Canada's former Prime Minister William Lyon Mackenzie King (pl. 4) as an example, saying that Mackenzie King was by no means a cooperative subject. "He invariably assumed that I should try to photograph the man that he visualized himself to be, rather than the man that I saw. He would explain carefully that he must not be interpreted incorrectly, or be shown to the people in a manner that would mislead them. It was never perfectly clear to me how he did visualize himself (I would have paid no more than polite attention to such desires anyway). He claimed to be a very modest person, and I believe that he considered that he was modest. I know that he liked to see in my interpretations of him some reflection of the missionary to mankind, of humility on his part, even a studied humility. If this comment about King seems particularly appropriate to some people, I must emphasize that I have rarely photographed a successful politician in active public life who did not clasp his hand against his chest and profess humility by pose or gesture, if not in so many words."[93]

And who has made as many portraits of power-holding politicians as Yousuf Karsh?

In dealing with power-holders and celebrities Karsh has been confronted by style. When Karsh went to photograph Marshal Tito he suggested how he should dress for the portrait. His advice was romantic: "I suggested a shirt with an open collar, such as a man of the people would wear. But that did not seem appropriate to him, and he put on a new blue Field Marshal's uniform."[94] Tito was wearing this uniform for the first time, to impress Karsh and the public, whose surrogate the photographer was.

But Karsh did, unconsciously, promote a style among some celebrities. When he photographed Albert Einstein, Einstein wore a sweater for the portrait (fig. 40). Some time later, Karsh arrived to photograph Pablo Casals (pl. 36) and found him "wearing a little sweater." Even Albert Schweitzer suggested wearing one after he had seen Karsh's picture of Einstein. "Ever since Einstein's picture," Karsh writes, "and even more since Hemingway's (pl. 25), I have difficulty in persuading certain of my subjects not to wear sweaters."[95]

In the case of Karsh himself, at a more profound level, the Comte de Buffon's "Le style est l'homme même" (the style is the man himself)[96] is an accurate insight. Karsh's survival, and his success in achieving the goals of his professional career, have been cardinally dependent upon the nature and quality of the style of his interpersonal skills. For Karsh, photography is a link with others, not just a means for self-expression. The accomplishments that these skills must effect are: contacting a celebrity, whether a busy head of state or an irascible creative genius, and gaining suitable access to him or her; successfully engaging the subject in exploratory dialogue; evoking from the subject the right "moment" for a photograph; effectively recording that moment with the lights and camera; and returning to re-photograph, if necessary or desired. The resulting portrait photograph, the one that Karsh selects and adds to his collection, is the incarnation of the quality of his interpersonal relationship with that particular subject – for all to see.

The style of any portrait photographer determines the style of the resulting portrait; they are inseparable, almost mirror images. If Karsh's clients, the subjects and potential subjects, the image-using media, or the public, had rejected Karsh's portraits – in the manner that Churchill rejected Graham Sutherland's portrait[97] – then, to put it bluntly, Karsh this past half century would have been exercising his photographic skills otherwise.

Karsh comments on his interpersonal style as a fifteen-year-old student in Canada: "Sometimes the teachers would make a little speech to the

134

class about how I came to be there, and how they should be polite to me at all times because I had the reputation of being unusually courteous myself. I knew that they were speaking about me, and saying gracious things about my manners, which I suspect have always erred in the direction of being overly polite."[98] Sixty-five years later Karsh comments: "I arrived in Canada armed with nothing but good manners." And ever since, he says, they have been the greatest guarantee of his career.[99] John F. Burns of *The New York Times* says that Karsh's claim of good manners is a much more modest accounting of a quality remarked upon by Karsh's friends as his grace. Bruce Ward, a staff writer for *The Ottawa Citizen*, quickly perceived Karsh's style while interviewing the eighty-year-old Karsh: "If sheer niceness and normality were the measure of greatness, Karsh would have yet another claim to immortality."[100] Burns goes on to note something that Karsh's friends have also learned: his rule "that graciousness should never lapse into timidity."[101]

Burns cites an example demonstrating both sides of Karsh. Regarding Karsh's well-known portrait of Nikita Khrushchev, Burns writes, "perhaps only Mr. Karsh would have had the daring – and the charm – to have persuaded the most powerful man in Soviet Russia to pose indoors, in the Moscow spring, in a woollen balaclava and a massive fur coat." Karsh told Khrushchev that he would like to make individual portraits of the entire Soviet leadership, but Khrushchev remonstrated with him by saying that, under the Soviet system, posing for a photograph was a decision for the individual members of the Presidium to make. "By the following morning," Burns writes, "miraculously, all the individuals had decided."[102]

Karsh's combination of commitment, talent for fame, photographic and interpersonal skills is unique. It is impossible to conclude otherwise, for, on the one hand, there are tens of thousands of competent photographers in the world, and, on the other hand, almost all of us are curious to see the faces of those who shape the world: there is a market for "portraits of greatness," and "faces of destiny." Yet Karsh is the only portrait photographer who is so well known and so frequently exhibited internationally. No other photographer has so laboured to put together a collection of portraits, and then so steadfastly worked for its public exposure through magazines, books, or exhibits. No other photographer has been so successful in hunting down and photographing the faces attached to household names.

There are some things Karsh will not do: "The question that . . . arises for me when I am photographing world-famous figures is whether I should record the legend, or something else about the personality that the public may be assumed not to know. I am satisfied that no purpose would be served if I were consciously to seek to convert what could be a portrait of greatness into a moment of weakness. Such moments are not worth recording. I admit that I am influenced by the public image, . . . by the living legend."[103]

For example, Karsh portrayed the Duke and Duchess of Windsor as a mutually admiring couple. "After viewing this photograph," Karsh writes, "the Duke and Duchess graciously wrote to me that I had captured their deep feelings for each other after thirty-four years of marriage."[104] In startling contrast, for example, is the view which Richard Avedon presents in his book *Observations*[105] of a tired, drained, bored, sad couple, lit by lighting appropriate for an operating theatre. The chasm between the styles exhibited in other portraits of the same subjects made by these two men – those of Somerset Maugham (pl. 27) or Marian Anderson, for instance – is unbridgeable.

There is another approach which Karsh rejects – that of startling the viewer. "[The photographer] can have them sit on cakes of ice, or he can have them climb trees," Karsh writes, "but these are not solutions for the portraitist, and I take some satisfaction from the fact that I have sought to minimize repetitiveness without resorting to such expedients."[106] Karsh is arguing against what might appear as formula portraiture, such as putting every person against the same backdrop, or introducing a surprising element that is repeated so often that it becomes a cliché unrelated to the subject – for example, the "jump shot" that the late Philippe Halsman took after every portrait sitting.[107]

Finally, Karsh does not sharply confront his clients and subjects, while photographer Irving Penn, for example, "takes an enormous number of photographs, and keeps on taking them until his subject, thinking that the ordeal of self-exposure is nearing the end, begins to lower his guard and permits his real image to appear. Sitting for a portrait by Penn is never an indifferent experience. He fences emotionally with his prey . . . he has to arouse the model . . . and he wilfully but gently takes charge."[108] Karsh likes to photograph his subjects, if possible, in their own environment, and strives to ensure that their experiences are such that they would subsequently welcome a visit by another photographer.

Karsh still works, and, just before his eightieth birthday, his wife Estrellita said that "he is happy, every day is a new adventure."[109] For he still loves his profession, and the results of his labours continue to bring worldwide attention and acclaim. In 1983, for example, a large exhibition of his portraits was presented at the International Center of Photography in New York, and is now being shown in the major cities of Europe. There is no doubt that Karsh, the man who "thrives on problems," has used his outstanding talents to achieve his life's goals of personal success and professional achievement. He has made a significant contribution to us all.

Today, we have his portraits before us; portraits of people possessing power of varying type and degree. And they remind us that the great person uses power in order to solve human problems and assuage human needs – including the need to be enlightened and to be entertained. His portraits meet our needs; not only our need to look closely at the great, but our need to be reminded that only by pursuing greatness can human hopes be realized.

Fig. 41
Man Ray (American, 1890–1976)
Yousuf Karsh 29 March 1965
Gelatin silver print
30.2 × 23.4 cm
Collection of the artist

Notes

The author acknowledges, with appreciation, the cooperation of the University of Toronto Press for permission to make extensive use of material from their publications.

1. Yousuf Karsh, *Karsh: A Fifty-Year Retrospective* (Toronto: The University of Toronto Press, 1983), p. 9.
2. Helmut Gernsheim, *Creative Photography: Aesthetic Trends 1839–1960* (London: Faber and Faber, 1962), p. 68.
3. Peter Pollack, *The Picture History of Photography: From the Earliest Beginnings to the Present Day* (New York: Harry N. Abrams, Inc., 1958), p. 498.
4. In 1946 Karsh was invited to attend a ceremony in Ottawa in order to receive Canadian citizen certificate number one; the ceremony was to mark the new Act of Citizenship passed by Canada's Parliament. Karsh writes: "However, I did not have very long to relish my dreams of glory of being the No. 1 citizen of my adopted land. Some of the members of the Cabinet decided that they should be honoured, and ultimately my No. 1 certificate went to none other than Prime Minister Mackenzie King himself. No. 10 came to me. However, if I hold my thumb over the zero I can still pretend I hold No. 1." Yousuf Karsh, *In Search of Greatness: Reflections of Yousuf Karsh* (Toronto: University of Toronto Press, 1962), pp. 191–92.
5. Karl Popper, *Unended Quest: An Intellectual Autobiography* (La Salle, Illinois: Open Court, 1976), p. 22.
6. Popper, p. 88.
7. Bryan Magee, *Philosophy and the Real World: An Introduction to Karl Popper*, rev. (La Salle, Illinois: Open Court, 1982), pp. 67–68.
8. Yousuf Karsh, "Portraits of Famous Musicians," *The American Annual of Photography* (Boston: American Photographic, 1949), p. 66.
9. *Turkey: Nagel's Encyclopedia Guide*, (Geneva: Nagel, 1984), p. 654.
10. Karsh, *In Search of Greatness*, p. 138.
11. Karsh, *In Search of Greatness*, p. 4.
12. Karsh, *A Fifty-Year Retrospective*, p. 7.
13. Karsh, *In Search of Greatness*, p. 138.
14. Karsh, *In Search of Greatness*, p. 12.
15. Karsh, *In Search of Greatness*, p. 12.
16. Karsh, *In Search of Greatness*, p. 10.
17. Karsh, *A Fifty-Year Retrospective*, p. 7.
18. Karsh, *In Search of Greatness*, p. 9.
19. Karsh, *In Search of Greatness*, pp. 21–22.
20. *Encyclopædia Britannica* (1966), II, p. 421 and XXII, p. 606.
21. Karsh, *In Search of Greatness*, pp. 13–14.
22. Karsh, *A Fifty-Year Retrospective*, p. 15.
23. Karsh, *In Search of Greatness*, p. 19.
24. Karsh, *In Search of Greatness*, p. 21.
25. Karsh, *In Search of Greatness*, p. 33.
26. Karsh, *In Search of Greatness*, pp. 22, 24.
27. Karsh, *In Search of Greatness*, p. 27.
28. Karsh, *In Search of Greatness*, p. 30.
29. Karsh, *In Search of Greatness*, pp. 34, 37.
30. Karsh, *In Search of Greatness*, p. 36.
31. Karsh, *In Search of Greatness*, p. 27.
32. Karsh, *In Search of Greatness*, p. 56.
33. Karsh, *In Search of Greatness*, p. 37.
34. Edward Steichen, *A Life in Photography* (Garden City, N.Y.: Doubleday, in coll. with the Museum of Modern Art, New York, 1963), facing pl. 95.
35. Discussion with J.W. Borcoman.
36. Discussion with photographer and filmmaker Grant Crabtree.
37. Karsh, *A Fifty-Year Retrospective*, pp. 128–29.
38. Steichen, facing pl. 112.
39. Karsh, *In Search of Greatness*, p. 101.
40. Beaumont Newhall, *The History of Photography: From 1839 to the present day*, rev. and enl. (New York: Museum of Modern Art, 1964), p. 64.
41. Gernsheim, *Creative Photography*, p. 234.
42. Philip J. Pocock, "Synge and the Photography of His Time," in *The Autobiography of J. M. Synge* (Dublin: The Dolmen Press, 1965).
43. Karsh, *A Fifty-Year Retrospective*, p. 9.
44. Erich Stenger, *The March of Photography* (London: Focal Press, 1958), p. 111.
45. Gernsheim, *Creative Photography*, pp. 180, 239. See also: Helmut Gernsheim in coll. with Alison Gernsheim, *The History of Photography; from the earliest use of the camera obscura in the eleventh century up to 1914* (New York: Oxford University Press, 1955), p. 356; and E.O. Hoppé, *Hundred Thousand Exposures* (London: Focal Press, [1945]).
46. C.E. Kenneth Mees, *From Dry Plates to Ektachrome Film: A Story of Photographic Research* (New York: Ziff-Davis, 1961).
47. Henri Cartier-Bresson, "Introduction" to *The Decisive Moment* (1952), in *Photographers on Photography*, Nathan Lyons (ed.) (Rochester, N. Y.: Prentice-Hall, in coll. with George Eastman House, 1966), pp. 42, 51.

48. Beaumont and Nancy Newhall (eds), *Masters of Photography* (New York: George Braziller, 1958), p. 160.
49. Cartier-Bresson, p. 46.
50. Max J. Friedlander, *Landscape, Portrait, Still-Life: Their Origin and Development* (New York: Schocken Books, 1963), p. 233.
51. Cartier-Bresson, p. 44.
52. Cartier-Bresson, p. 42.
53. Cartier-Bresson, p. 43.
54. Karsh, *In Search of Greatness*, p. 166.
55. Eugene Smith was a panelist at an international photographic symposium held in Montreal at Expo 67 in 1967, under the sponsorship of the Thomas More Institute of Montreal. Other panelists were: L. Fritz Gruber (in charge of cultural exhibitions at Photokina in Cologne); Yousuf Karsh; Hans Lehman (a Montreal psychiatrist); Wayne Miller (a Magnum photographer and Edward Steichen's assistant during the creation of *The Family of Man* exhibition); Beaumont Newhall (director of the George Eastman House, Rochester, New York); Eric O'Connor (mathematician and president of the Thomas More Institute); and Philip J. Pocock (director of *The Camera as Witness* Expo 67 exhibition, and photographic advisor for the Canadian pavilion).
56. Albert Camus, *The Fall*, Justin O'Brien (trans.) (New York: Alfred A. Knopf, 1957).
57. Discussion with Grace M. Mayer, a long-time associate of Edward Steichen; she was Curator of the Department of Photography at the Museum of Modern Art, New York, when Edward Steichen was Director of the Department of Photography of the Museum.
58. In 1988, copies of *The New Yorker* frequently contained this ad: "Portraits by YOUSUF KARSH of Ottawa, in New York by appointment (212-838-4565) or Ottawa (613-236-7181)."
59. *Encyclopædia Britannica* (Micropædia, 1973), IX, p. 290.
60. *Encyc. Brit.*, V, p. 716.
61. Pollack, p. 498.
62. Gernsheim, *Creative Photography*, p. 68.
63. Discussion in New York with Charles Reynolds, photography consultant and editor, who was a colleague of Smith's for many years.
64. John Szarkowski, *Mirrors and Windows: American Photography Since 1960* (New York: Museum of Modern Art, 1978), p. 13.
65. John Szarkowski, *Looking at Photographs: 100 Pictures from the Collection of the Museum of Modern Art* (New York: Museum of Modern Art, 1973), p. 150.
66. Karsh, *In Search of Greatness*, p. 79.
67. "Karsh Chronology," unpublished, National Gallery of Canada, 1988.
68. Karsh, *In Search of Greatness*, p. 121.
69. W. Eugene Smith, photoessay "Pittsburgh," *1959 Photography Annual* (New York: Ziff-Davis, 1958).
70. See W. Eugene Smith and Aileen M. Smith, *Minimata* (New York: Holt, Rinehart and Winston, 1975).
71. Karsh, *In Search of Greatness*, p. 115.
72. G.K. Chesterton, *The Napoleon of Notting Hill* (Harmondsworth, Middlesex, and New York: Penguin Books, 1946), p. 18.
73. An expression of J.F. Martin of Ottawa.
74. Karsh, *In Search of Greatness*, p. viii.
75. Yousuf Karsh, *Portraits of Greatness* (Toronto: University of Toronto Press, 1959), p. 11.
76. Jean Alazard, *The Florentine Portrait* (New York: Schocken Books, [1968]), pp. 54, 59.
77. Karsh, *In Search of Greatness*, pp. 144–45.
78. Karsh, *In Search of Greatness*, p. 155.
79. Karsh, *In Search of Greatness*, p. 142.
80. Karsh, *In Search of Greatness*, p. 8.
81. A Canadianized version of *This Is the Mass* was made with Karsh photographing Cardinal Léger (whose brother Jules became Canada's Governor General) saying the mass in 1960. "Karsh Chronology."
82. Karsh, *In Search of Greatness*, pp. 93–94.
83. Karsh, *In Search of Greatness*, p. 131.
84. Karsh, *In Search of Greatness*, p. 130.
85. Yousuf Karsh, *Faces of Destiny* (Toronto: University of Toronto Press, 1946).
86. John F. Burns, "Yousuf Karsh and the Art of Friendly Persuasion," *The New York Times*, 1 January 1989, p. 31.
87. Yousuf Karsh, "Superlative Personalities," *The American Annual of Photography* (Boston: 1946), p. 19.
88. Karsh, *Portraits of Greatness*, p. 122.
89. Thomas Mann, *Lotte in Weimar*, published in the United States as *The Beloved Returns* (New York: Vintage Trade Books, 1983), pp. 290, 292.
90. Quoted by Richard Winston in *Thomas Mann: The Making of an Artist, 1875–1911* (New York: Alfred A. Knopf, 1981), p. 49.
91. Karsh, *Portraits of Greatness*, p. 12.
92. Karsh, *In Search of Greatness*, p. 14.
93. Karsh, *In Search of Greatness*, p. 83.
94. Karsh, *In Search of Greatness*, p. 149.

95. Karsh, *In Search of Greatness*, p. 157.

96. *Le style est l'homme même* is an address that Georges Louis Leclerc, Comte de Buffon, gave to the Académie Française on 25 August 1753.

97. The most celebrated recent case of a rejected portrait is that of Winston Churchill's by Graham Sutherland, who had become known for doing portraits which were acclaimed as expressionistic and penetrating; "Somerset Maugham" (1949, Tate Gallery) was the first of the series. The British Parliament commissioned Sutherland to do Churchill's portrait in honour of his eightieth birthday. Churchill so disliked Sutherland's portrait that he forbade either its exhibition or reproduction; it was subsequently destroyed.

98. Karsh, *In Search of Greatness*, p. 16.

99. Quoted by Burns, p. 31.

100. Bruce Ward, "Karsh: Photographer Still Going Strong at 80," *The Ottawa Citizen*, 17 December 1988, p. C1.

101. Burns, p. 31.

102. Burns, p. 34.

103. Karsh, *In Search of Greatness*, p. 101.

104. Karsh, *A Fifty-Year Retrospective*, p. 18.

105. Richard Avedon, *Observations*, comments by Truman Capote [New York: Simon and Schuster, 1959].

106. Karsh, *In Search of Greatness*, p. 114.

107. After every portrait sitting Philippe Halsman asked the sitter to jump in the air, and his photos of these jumping sitters, including for example Richard Nixon and the Duke of Windsor, were published in his "jump book."

108. Alexander Liberman, in the "Introduction" to Irving Penn, *Moments Preserved: Eight Essays in Photographs and Words* (New York: Simon and Schuster, 1960), pp. 9–11.

109. Ward, page C1.

The Karsh Collection

Lilly Koltun

In 1987, the National Archives of Canada acquired the works of Yousuf Karsh, totalling some 355,000 negatives, prints and transparencies. This massive corpus comprises a virtually intact record of Karsh's activity as a photographer from 1933, his first full year in business in Ottawa, to March 31, 1987, the date of the acquisition. Thus it represents not only an exhaustive set of the distilled final images regarded as the product of his artistic talent, but also the entire surviving context within which the images were created.

In acquiring the Karsh Collection, the National Archives is fulfilling its role as the repository of significant cultural archives for the country, those of artists as much as of politicians, authors, and other historically important figures. Beyond facilitating the study of an internationally significant artist in Canadian society, the collection also responds to the special role of the National Archives of Canada as the repository of the National Portrait Collection. The National Portrait Collection program was consolidated some twenty years ago in recognition of the unparalleled existing portrait holdings in the documentary art and photography collections which had grown up since the founding of the National Archives in 1872. Through the program, the Archives has acquired pictures of individuals from every part of society, dating from the sixteenth century to the present day. The detailed series of over 10,530 sittings in the Karsh acquisition add

an impressive swath of the famous, rich and powerful, as well as of the less well-known, to this repository.

The Karsh Collection in itself exhibits a documentary density that may serve a multiplicity of future research needs. For example, the clientele for the portraits, although varied, in general represent the well-to-do and famous. The collection carves a fifty-five-year slice from that social stratum at both the national and international levels. This offers a rich resource for sociological, historical and statistical interpretation. The most cursory glance at the images exposes how much more the camera has captured than the faces of the sitters: the fashions in make-up and clothing, the roles of props and surroundings, the attitudes and poses struck, the intention to define a certain kind of public identity for posterity. The exhaustive nature of the Karsh Collection allows comparative analysis: between one photograph and another, between recent works and those of the past. What has been copied or invented, what inserted or omitted, what given new or different emphasis? Such comparisons reveal not only the thought processes and intentions of the artist dissecting and reconstructing images, but the age, the environment and the purposes within which both photographer and client operated.

The very volume of the material – all the negatives and transparencies Karsh created during his career until March 31, 1987, are the property of the Archives – offers archival value in itself, because it allows not only a present-day assessment of Karsh and the society documented, but also the possibility of extensive and in depth reassessment in the future. In general, the more significant the creator or comprehensive the social document, the more inevitable and frequent will be the reassessment; hence, the more crucial is the volume retained by the archivist.

The Karsh Collection's fine captions, including exact dates for the sittings, are a further aid to this historical research, as is the exercise which Karsh performed in 1982, when he reviewed the collection and separated into individually marked envelopes the negatives from each portrait sitting which he then judged the best, quite apart from those the client had previously selected.

All this is to say why the Karsh Collection is so happily housed in the National Archives of Canada. It responds to every important selection criterion: its creator and content are of national significance on many fronts; its scope has the virtue of comprehensiveness and the potential for multiple research use; its contents are well organized and well documented; it has a close relationship with existing holdings; and, as a repository documenting a Canadian's outstanding achievement in the medium of photography, it is of formidable rarity.

The researcher surveying the collection in more detail is struck first by the impressive size of Karsh's professional practice: approximately 136,000 large format black-and-white negatives, together with 16,500 items in the colour collection. As well, there are some 65,500 prints in the collection, including the 15,800 "deluxe" vintage prints, and the "Famous 500" – Karsh's own specially printed selection of his chosen best.

In fact, these negatives and transparencies do not represent quite all of Karsh's work as, in 1972 when he moved his studio, he reviewed the collection and culled and destroyed the results of some 2,522 sittings, together with selected negatives from others.

Allowing for these, Karsh completed on average about 250 portrait assignments each year over his career. A limited sampling indicates that about 59 per cent of the collection represents Canadian sittings and about 41 per cent is international. Karsh maintained a staff and studio in Ottawa and operated through agents in New York and London. In addition, he undertook some commissioned editorial and commercial work.

The trend of the entire collection is already perceptible within the first year's production. Karsh once remembered his early work, before the landmark publication of his famous Winston Churchill portrait (frontispiece) on the cover of *Saturday Night* in 1942, as a time when 90 per cent of his work was photographs of women. Analysis of his first twelve months' worth of work, totalling 534 glass and celluloid negatives in the cumbersome and challenging 8×10 and 5×7 inch formats, reveals that some 42 per cent of his photographs are of women; 31 per cent are of men; and 2 per cent are of couples; leaving 25 per cent to be divided among the photographer's staples of children, weddings, groups, passport photographs and commercial work.

From the moment he numbered his first envelope of negatives on 25 April 1933 as a young man of twenty-four, Karsh attracted a clientele which competed very favourably in numbers and economic level with the thirteen other established photographic studios listed in the Ottawa city directory for that year. Among Karsh's clients, the single women can seldom be associated with careers; however, the men include a healthy representation from business and the professions: military men, lawyers, doctors, accountants, government and bank employees, dentists, engineers, managers, businessmen, and a judge. Karsh also attracted commissions from the British High Commissioner William H. Clark and his wife Anne

Elizabeth Clark, the Chinese Consul C. Chou, the architect W. Edgar Noffke, and the Senator W.A. Buchanan.

This is all the more remarkable as so many of the other studios were long-established: not only that of John Powis (whose studio address he assumed after working for him briefly as an assistant), but also the Hands Studio, and those of Paul Horsdal, J. Alex Castonguay (who photographed Karsh in 1936 with Karsh returning the favour in 1959), and Percy Hardy (successor to the Pittaway and Jarvis firm, founded in 1882). The representative work by these men in the holdings of the National Archives of Canada, encompassing the bulk of the studio production of Castonguay (fig. 42) and Horsdal, reveals a substantial client base and a style comparable to that absorbed by the young Karsh (see fig. 31). (Indeed the study of the Karsh family of photographers is facilitated at the National Archives where there are also large selections from the works of Nakash (George Nakashian), who was Karsh's uncle and early mentor, and of Malak, Karsh's brother.)

The very first twenty envelopes in the entire sequence of negatives in the collection portray the cast and productions of the Dominion Drama Festival, which was founded in 1933 and for which Karsh was appointed official photographer. The earliest surviving finished vintage print in the collection is from negative number 9, and shows Lysle Courtenay (pl. 5) posed according to venerable artistic tradition by a tall window in what might be a study, but is in actuality the Festival office. Such classical settings, with their presentation of a dignified figure in a library or study setting, appear throughout Karsh's work, for example in his sequence of Paul Claudel (fig. 43). Recognition by researchers of such structured compositions is essential in understanding the documentary information carried by the image which is being produced in answer both

143

Fig. 42
J.A. Castonguay (Canadian, 1877–1972)
Charles Marchand 1937
Bromoil print
24.0 × 17.4 cm
National Archives of Canada, PA-165835

Fig. 43
Yousuf Karsh
Paul Claudel 8 July 1954
Gelatin silver, printed later
24.7 × 19.6 cm
National Archives of Canada, PA-170169

to Karsh's stylistic control and to the client's requirements.

Over the following twelve months there are further assignments linked to the stage world (fig. 44), including a visit by the Festival group to the Governor General's residence in April 1934. Each April through to 1937 Karsh photographed the Festival group again. Many of his first professional contacts with the well-known seem to have come from these theatrical commissions. He photographed, among others, Robert Borden (fig. 45), former prime minister and now president of the Festival Committee; the Governor General, Lord Bessborough, patron; and Duncan Campbell Scott (fig. 46), Canadian poet and author, who supported the Ottawa Little Theatre as well as the Dominion Drama Festival.

His "first winning photo" (note on the envelope), a 1926 pictorial landscape, shows, in soft focus, a wooded path by a stream with children, and is recorded in the collection by a copy negative and modern prints (see fig. 31). After his apprenticeship with the well-known photographer John H. Garo of Boston, his portraits display a concern for more focussed content and design, but remain within the traditional context illustrated by the Lysle Courtenay portrait. The image of Anne Elizabeth Clark in 1934 (fig. 47) shows the development of the elements which were to become Karsh's trademark: the dramatic surface pattern (here created through a high background arch behind the profile of Anne Clark and the frontal pose of the dog), the artificial light and studio calm, and the fine-grained realism rendered possible by the technical capacity of the large negative and camera and enhanced by retouching.

During this period, occasional "experimental" negatives appear in the collection. Icicles (fig. 48), architectural elements, repetitive shapes like straws or ice cream cones, all provide opportunities for the studied interplay of individual forms combined in a surface pattern. Photographs of the

Fig. 44
Yousuf Karsh
Ottawa Little Theatre: "Les Sœurs
Guedonec" 22 April 1936
Gelatin silver, printed later
24.1 × 31.8 cm
National Archives of Canada, PA-165836

Fig. 45
Yousuf Karsh
Robert Borden 25 October 1933
Gelatin silver, printed later
50.5 × 40.4 cm
National Archives of Canada, PA-165852

145

Fig. 46
Yousuf Karsh
Duncan Campbell Scott 16 September 1933
Gelatin silver, printed later
26.5 × 32.1 cm
National Archives of Canada, PA-165842

Fig. 47
Yousuf Karsh
Lady Clark, with Angus 9 August 1934
Matte gelatin silver print
23.5 × 18.8 cm
National Archives of Canada, PA-165834

146

light and shadow patterns thrown over the stairs of the Peace Tower of the Parliament Buildings, taken in 1935, parallel similar explorations of Karsh's contemporaries, including Ottawans Clifford Johnston (whose *Design*, 1934, was also based on the Parliament Buildings), and Johan Helders. Indeed, Karsh's connections with contemporary Canadians and the "artistic photography" movement in this country is an unexplored area of his career. In the 1930s, the National Gallery of Canada was the site of an annual Canadian International Salon of Photographic Art where Helders, for example, was a judge. Karsh's portrait of Helders of 1938 (pl. 1) shows him with one of Karsh's own experimental landscapes from the *Icicles* series.

In addition, the collection contains some little-known experimentation from the 1930s of neo-classical inspiration, with nudes or semi-nudes in windblown "Grecian" drapery, another link with his contemporaries like Harold Kells. One of these images, a 1938 photograph entitled *Spring Song* (fig. 49) is of his future wife Solange Gauthier. After her death in 1961, he used the image as the inspiration for the design of a prize medal to be awarded annually in a playwriting competition by the Ottawa Little Theatre.

The collection documents both the tools Karsh used to achieve his effects and how they changed over time: the "red coccine" washes used to control densities and tonal values in the earlier negatives, such as the Pablo Picasso portraits; the retouching (where a client's wish to appear younger might have been communicated to a technician with the note "without over-exaggeration"); the masks and cropping; the tissue-sketches to assist composition; the invisible spotting of prints; the instructions for colour balancing, dodging and burning. One technique for which we may be grateful is the use of selenium or gold toning to finish prints. These highly effective methods to conserve black-and-

Fig. 48
Yousuf Karsh
Icicles 1938
Gelatin silver, printed later
19.3 × 18.9 cm
National Archives of Canada, PA-170171

white images have rendered Karsh's deluxe prints of outstanding keeping quality. He made a speciality also of formats unusual to other photographers: enormous 30 × 40 inch prints, or prints on rare papers, such as certain difficult and now discontinued matte papers like Opal V (pl. 36).

The importance of the translation from negative to final print is clear in the Karsh Collection. Making allowance for technical problems such as the unavailability of original papers, it is nonetheless noteworthy that technicians find it difficult to produce a "Karsh" quality print even from the original negative without the guidance of an existing print or of Karsh himself.

Among the most intriguing of the transformations from negative to positive is the preparation of multiple negatives superimposed to create one image during printing. This technique was used for portraits, for example the placing of Picasso beside a vase, and for commercial and advertising work which, although infrequent, does occur in the collection. The commission for Atlas Steels Company in 1950 inspired a series of heroic interior scenes, with workers superimposed in the foreground (fig. 50). Another series of 1950s advertisements superimposed a happy couple, a car called the "Willys" and a spotlight on the scene.

Karsh won at least two awards for his "commercial and editorial" work, one from the Art Directors' Club of Chicago in 1950 and one from the Art Directors' Club of Montreal in 1955. These assignments however, like the routine work of weddings, disappear from Karsh's commercial work sometime in the 1960s, although he continued to do portraits and accept commissions from magazines or other publishers.

Over 1952–54, Karsh accepted an assignment from *Maclean's* magazine to photograph first ten, then another six, of Canada's major cities. The night scene on Granville Street in Vancouver (fig. 51) required not only a B.C. Electric hydraulic

Fig. 49
Yousuf Karsh
Spring Song (Solange Gauthier) 1938
Gelatin silver, printed later
50.3 × 40.3 cm
National Archives of Canada, PA-165837

Fig. 50
Yousuf Karsh
Atlas Steels, Welland, Ontario
26–30 June 1950
Gelatin silver print
49.5 × 39.1 cm
National Archives of Canada, PA-165854

Fig. 51
Yousuf Karsh
*Granville Street, Vancouver, British
Columbia* 1952
Gelatin silver print
27.3 × 34.3 cm
National Archives of Canada, PA-165855
For the *Maclean's* assignment "Face of
Canada"

149

platform for the exposures, but also a sandwich of no fewer than six 8 × 10 inch retouched negatives superimposed on each other, in order to print all the neon. This print is one of the most deliberately "designed" images in the entire collection.

The negatives in the collection which deal with this series total 8,334, with an additional 378 colour transparencies and about 8,500 red proofs and prints. Of these, the magazine's editor selected 280 black-and-white and twenty-two colour images in all. The effect of such editorial selection must be carefully weighed in any attempt to define, distill or judge a body of work known only through selected sources rather than the archival whole.

It is the black-and-white portraiture which is Karsh's best-known work. The collection in the National Archives of Canada, however, also contains some 16,500 colour transparencies. He appears to have begun using colour about 1947, around the time he photographed William Lyon Mackenzie King using 8 × 10 inch colour transparency film. Subsequently, he would expose colour as well as black-and-white during some sittings. These instances are not always indicated on his file cards. The colour transparencies were stored separately, alphabetically according to the name of the sitter, with no consistent cross-reference to the chronological sequence of the black-and-white material. They reveal themselves as surprising counterpoints to certain sittings in the collection. The reinterpretation of a subject in colour requires a fine balance of optical vibration among demanding, often contrasting, colours, compared to the subtle tonal gradations of the single range between black-and-white extremes.

Although, as with his black-and-white work, Karsh usually used large format colour transparencies (8 × 10, 5 × 7 and 4 × 5 inch), there are some smaller format pieces. There are also some colour and black-and-white instant print photographs starting as early as 1958, which he used to test his results during sittings prior to making the final exposures.

Karsh's transparencies were used in a variety of ways. Magazines such as *Maclean's, Collier's* and *Life* requested them for reproduction purposes. At times, Karsh created black-and-white prints from transparencies. Or they became the basis for the highly costly creation of colour separations in 11 × 14 and 16 × 20 inch sizes, from which dye transfer prints were produced for clients. Colour separations and dye transfer prints represented two of the very few stable colour processes, ensuring that at least certain selected Karsh photographs would retain their integrity and colour balance within possibly the optimum known colour technology of the time. Nothing less could be allowed out of the Karsh studio to be delivered to the Queen of England, the Governor General or the Pope. The collection in the National Archives contains some hundreds of these colour separations and preliminary dye transfer prints, the latter's brilliant jewel-like dyes glistening on the paper in variations which reveal the care required to balance the colours for the final result. Karsh worked with the Evans Color Laboratory in New York to produce these images.

Unfortunately, other parts of the colour collection did not survive the years as well, and colour shift has made a number of the earlier images magenta in tone, apparently leading Karsh to dispose of selected transparencies.

Not all, however, have lost their power. Among the most effective are those Karsh did for the movies. As part of his commercial work, he produced stills for *Sodom and Gomorrah* (1961), *Zulu* (1963), and *Planet of the Apes* (1967), in both black-and-white and colour. Karsh's colour transparencies still retain a clear intensity of hue and, for *Zulu* (fig. 52, fig. 53), the results of the brilliant on-location sunlight. The attempt by the filmmakers of *Zulu* to be historically accurate allowed Karsh to film Africans on the set,

151

Fig. 52
Yousuf Karsh
*"Zulu": Ulla Jacobsson, with
Extras* June–July 1963
Gelatin silver, printed 1989
40.8 × 39.8 cm
Collection of the artist

Fig. 53
Yousuf Karsh
"Zulu": Extra June–July 1963
Gelatin silver, printed 1989
40.0 × 39.3 cm
Collection of the artist

descendants of the original Zulu who battled the British at Rorke's Drift in Natal, Africa, in 1879, including the young chief M.G. Buthelezi.

Finally, the collection includes about 2,000 photographs of Karsh himself, receiving awards, at the openings of his exhibitions and launchings of his books, lecturing, on the road, at home, with his family, and in the studio, taken some by himself, some by the young photographers he had as assistants in his studio, and some by friends, publicists, journalists and students.

The colour work, the commercial work, the relationship of Karsh to the Canadian photographic community, the detailed comparison of original negative with original positive, or of all the negatives and prints in a sequence, or of the contemporary prints against the "selected" negatives chosen as best in 1982 – all these remain largely unexamined. In the archival collection the potential source material for such exploration is preserved.

It has been said that, "when history reaches out for an understanding of the great men and women of our time, it will use Karsh portraits."[*] If so, the Karsh Collection acquired by the National Archives of Canada serves history well in preserving evidence of how one clear-seeing heart and mind has found and interpreted our humanity.

[*]As quoted in the introduction to the exhibition catalogue for *Men Who Make Our World* (Alberta: Government of Alberta and the Glenbow Museum, 12 November 1976 to 2 January 1977), n.p.

Catalogue

In dimensions, height precedes width.

Ansel Adams 20 July 1977
Gelatin silver print
22.0 × 16.5 cm
National Archives of Canada, PA-165831

Konrad Adenauer 12 June 1964
Gelatin silver print (emulsion-texture-enhanced)
25.9 × 31.6 cm
National Archives of Canada, PA-165801

Josef Albers 4 July 1966
Matte gelatin silver, printed 1987
21.2 × 21.6 cm
National Gallery of Canada
Gift of the artist

Muhammad Ali's Hands 27 March 1970
Matte gelatin silver, printed 1988
37.3 × 39.5 cm
National Gallery of Canada
Gift of the artist

Wilbur J. Allen 11 May 1966
Gelatin silver print
26.0 × 33.0 cm
National Archives of Canada, PA-165884

Donald B. Anderson 21 April 1964
Gelatin silver print (emulsion-texture-enhanced)
32.8 × 25.5 cm
National Archives of Canada, PA-165845

Elizabeth Arden 13 February 1948
Matte gelatin silver, printed 1988
35.0 × 27.2 cm
National Gallery of Canada
Gift of the artist

Atlas Steels, Welland, Ontario 26–30 June 1950
Gelatin silver print
49.5 × 39.1 cm
National Archives of Canada, PA-165854

Atlas Steels, Welland, Ontario: Steelworker
    26–30 June 1950
Gelatin silver print
34.0 × 26.9 cm
National Archives of Canada, PA-165853

Atlas Steels, Welland, Ontario: Kenneth (Tiny)
    Stirtzinger 26–30 June 1950
Gelatin silver print
26.7 × 27.3 cm
National Archives of Canada, PA-165829

Atlas Steels, Welland, Ontario: Timekeeper
    26–30 June 1950
Gelatin silver print
19.4 × 24.1 cm
National Archives of Canada, PA-165898

153

W.H. Auden 30 October 1972
Matte gelatin silver, printed 1988
27.5 × 19.8 cm
National Gallery of Canada
Gift of the artist

Jean-Louis Barrault 28 May 1949
Matte gelatin silver, printed 1988
50.3 × 39.6 cm
National Gallery of Canada
Gift of the artist

Joseph Baum 15 November 1959
Gelatin silver print (emulsion-texture-enhanced)
32.6 × 25.9 cm
National Archives of Canada, PA-165892

William Benton 13 April 1959
Gelatin silver print (emulsion-texture-enhanced)
23.5 × 19.8 cm
National Archives of Canada, PA-165858

Ingrid Bergman 24 February 1946
Matte gelatin silver, printed 1989
50.7 × 40.7 cm
Collection of the artist

Ernest Bevin 12 September–12 November 1943
Gelatin silver print
39.7 × 31.7 cm
National Archives of Canada, PA-165913

Walter Bloor 1 May 1947
Gelatin silver print (emulsion-texture-enhanced)
24.2 × 19.0 cm
National Archives of Canada, PA-165880

Robert Borden 25 October 1933
Gelatin silver, printed later
50.5 × 40.4 cm
National Archives of Canada, PA-165852

*Kenneth M. Brinkhous, Robert D. Langdell, and
   Robert H. Wagner* 16 May 1978
Gelatin silver print
26.0 × 32.9 cm
National Archives of Canada, PA-165802

John Buchan 27 October 1938
Gelatin silver print (emulsion-texture-enhanced)
32.8 × 26.0 cm
National Archives of Canada, PA-165803

*John Buchan (Lord Tweedsmuir), William Lyon
   Mackenzie King, Franklin D. Roosevelt, and
   James Roosevelt, Quebec City* 31 July 1936
Gelatin silver, printed 1988
23.7 × 18.6 cm
National Gallery of Canada
Gift of the artist

Edmond H. Caddy 18 June 1969
Gelatin silver print (emulsion-texture-enhanced)
32.9 × 26.0 cm
National Archives of Canada, PA-165881

Pablo Casals 30 June–1 July 1954
Gelatin silver (emulsion-texture-enhanced),
   printed later
27.7 × 21.6 cm
National Archives of Canada, PA-165804

James E. Casey 12 January 1960
Gelatin silver print (emulsion-texture-enhanced)
32.9 × 26.2 cm
National Archives of Canada, PA-165883

Fidel Castro 1 August 1971
Gelatin silver, printed 1988
49.7 × 40.3 cm
National Gallery of Canada
Gift of the artist

Marc Chagall 20 September 1965
Gelatin silver, printed 1987
39.7 × 43.0 cm
National Gallery of Canada
Gift of the artist

Leon Charash 5 September 1980
Gelatin silver print
35.3 × 27.9 cm
National Archives of Canada, PA-165805

Madame Chiang Kai-shek 15 June 1943
Matte gelatin silver, printed later
28.0 × 20.2 cm
National Archives of Canada, PA-165915

Thomas D. Church 10 December 1960
Gelatin silver print
34.2 × 21.1 cm
National Archives of Canada, PA-165926

Winston Churchill 30 December 1941
Gelatin silver, printed 1988
50.2 × 40.7 cm
National Gallery of Canada
Gift of the artist

Winston Churchill 30 December 1941
Gelatin silver (emulsion-texture-enhanced),
    printed later
27.8 × 21.7 cm
National Archives of Canada, PA-165806

René Clair 26 June 1954
Gelatin silver, printed 1988
49.0 × 39.2 cm
National Gallery of Canada
Gift of the artist

Lady Clark, with Angus 9 August 1934
Matte gelatin silver print
23.5 × 18.8 cm
National Archives of Canada, PA-165834

Jean Cocteau 9 July 1949
Gelatin silver, printed later
40.6 × 30.8 cm
National Archives of Canada, PA-165910

Katharine Cornell 20 February 1947
Matte gelatin silver, printed later
49.3 × 39.5 cm
National Archives of Canada, PA-165808

Lysle Courtenay 25 April 1933
Matte gelatin silver print
25.0 × 20.0 cm
National Archives of Canada, PA-165833

Noël Coward 12 September–12 November 1943
Gelatin silver, printed later
32.2 × 25.8 cm
National Archives of Canada, PA-165919

Joan Crawford 2 December 1948
Gelatin silver, printed later
48.4 × 38.5 cm
National Archives of Canada, PA-165909

Thomas S. Cullen 12 January 1947
Gelatin silver, printed later
50.6 × 40.9 cm
National Archives of Canada, PA-165924

Robertson Davies 10 October 1956
Gelatin silver print (emulsion-texture-enhanced)
24.1 × 19.1 cm
National Archives of Canada, PA-165875

Robertson Davies 4 November 1977
Matte gelatin silver, printed 1989
24.2 × 19.1 cm
Collection of the artist

Bette Davis 9 February 1946
Gelatin silver print (emulsion-texture-enhanced)
27.5 × 20.7 cm
National Archives of Canada, PA-165923

Michael E. DeBakey 16 February 1969
Matte gelatin silver, printed 1989
40.4 × 35.6 cm
Collection of the artist

Cecil B. deMille 21 March 1956
Matte gelatin silver, printed 1988
39.9 × 47.8 cm
National Gallery of Canada
Gift of the artist

Gérard Depardieu 16 October 1985
Gelatin silver print
25.3 × 19.0 cm
National Archives of Canada, PA-165809

Christian Dior 26 June 1954
Matte gelatin silver, printed 1988
27.6 × 21.4 cm
National Gallery of Canada
Gift of the artist

Ruth Draper 25 November 1936
Matte gelatin silver, printed 1989
48.6 × 36.9 cm
Collection of the artist

Albert Einstein 11 February 1948
Gelatin silver (emulsion-texture-enhanced),
    printed later
24.0 × 19.2 cm
National Archives of Canada, PA-165851

Dwight D. Eisenhower 20 July 1966
Gelatin silver print
24.1 × 19.1 cm
National Archives of Canada, PA-165890

John Enders 18 March 1975
Gelatin silver print (emulsion-texture-enhanced)
24.1 × 19.0 cm
National Archives of Canada, PA-165879

Georges Enesco 4 June 1954
Gelatin silver, printed later
42.9 × 34.4 cm
National Archives of Canada, PA-165810

Jacob Epstein 10 December 1955
Matte gelatin silver, printed 1987
50.3 × 39.5 cm
National Gallery of Canada
Gift of the artist

"Face of Canada": *Calgary Stampede* July 1953
Matte gelatin silver print
13.2 × 18.0 cm
National Archives of Canada, PA-165899
For the *Maclean's* assignment

"Face of Canada": *Mary Fatt of Fort Resolution,
    Charles Camsell Hospital, Edmonton* 1952
Matte gelatin silver print
29.3 × 26.2 cm
National Archives of Canada, PA-165897
For the *Maclean's* assignment

"Face of Canada": *Garrison Club, Quebec
    City* 1953
Matte gelatin silver print
33.0 × 26.7 cm
National Archives of Canada, PA-165812
For the *Maclean's* assignment

"Face of Canada": *Camillien Houde,
    Montreal* October 1952
Gelatin silver print (emulsion-texture-enhanced)
19.9 × 25.5 cm
National Archives of Canada, PA-165816
For the *Maclean's* assignment

"Face of Canada": *Roderick MacDonald,
    Charlottetown* 1952
Gelatin silver print
18.8 × 24.2 cm
National Archives of Canada, PA-165867
For the *Maclean's* assignment

"Face of Canada": *Daniel Makokis,
    Edmonton* 1952
Gelatin silver print
27.2 × 20.3 cm
National Archives of Canada, PA-165938
For the *Maclean's* assignment

"Face of Canada": *Quebec City* 1953
Gelatin silver, printed 1989
41.0 × 39.9 cm
Collection of the artist
For the *Maclean's* assignment

"Face of Canada": *Saint John, New
    Brunswick* 1952
Gelatin silver, printed 1989
40.0 × 39.3 cm
Collection of the artist
For the *Maclean's* assignment

"Face of Canada": *Saint John, New
    Brunswick* 1952
Gelatin silver, printed 1989
40.5 × 39.7 cm
Collection of the artist
For the *Maclean's* assignment

"Face of Canada": *Saint John, New
    Brunswick* 1952
Gelatin silver, printed 1989
40.9 × 39.8 cm
Collection of the artist
For the *Maclean's* assignment

"Face of Canada": *Herman Sattler, Saskatchewan
    Wheat Farmer* 1952
Gelatin silver print
26.1 × 34.1 cm
National Archives of Canada, PA-165900
For the *Maclean's* assignment

"Face of Canada": *TB Patients, Charles Camsell
    Hospital, Edmonton* 1952
Matte gelatin silver print
26.7 × 26.3 cm
National Archives of Canada, PA-165896
For the *Maclean's* assignment

Mel Ferrer's Hands 23 March 1956
Matte gelatin silver, printed 1989
24.8 × 31.9 cm
Collection of the artist

Ford Canada, Windsor 5–15 February 1951
Matte gelatin silver, printed 1989
39.1 × 48.8 cm
Collection of the artist

Ford Canada, Windsor: Paint Shop
    5–15 February 1951
Matte gelatin silver, printed 1988
40.1 × 49.6 cm
National Gallery of Canada
Gift of the artist

Robert Frost 4 April 1958
Gelatin silver (emulsion-texture-enhanced),
    printed later
27.8 × 21.6 cm
National Archives of Canada, PA-165901

R. Buckminster Fuller 22 May 1980
Matte gelatin silver, printed 1988
35.0 × 27.1 cm
National Gallery of Canada
Gift of the artist

Clark Gable 1 December 1948
Gelatin silver print (emulsion-texture-enhanced)
32.3 × 25.9 cm
National Archives of Canada, PA-165811

Frank Gannett 9 September 1953
Gelatin silver print (emulsion-texture-enhanced)
32.9 × 27.3 cm
National Archives of Canada, PA-165862

John H. Garo 1931
Gelatin silver, printed later
26.7 × 31.6 cm
National Archives of Canada, PA-165838

Charles de Gaulle 11 July 1944
Matte gelatin silver, printed 1988
50.1 × 38.3 cm
National Gallery of Canada
Gift of the artist

Gratien Gélinas 29 March 1945
Gelatin silver print
24.0 × 19.1 cm
National Archives of Canada, PA-165888

J. Paul Getty 20 May 1964
Gelatin silver print (emulsion-texture-enhanced)
32.8 × 26.1 cm
National Archives of Canada, PA-165813

Valéry Giscard d'Estaing 21 March 1981
Matte gelatin silver, printed 1988
35.0 × 27.3 cm
National Gallery of Canada
Gift of the artist

John Graham 13 May 1971
Gelatin silver print (emulsion-texture-enhanced)
32.8 × 26.2 cm
National Archives of Canada, PA-165864

Aurèle Gratton 23 August 1965
Gelatin silver print (emulsion-texture-enhanced)
32.9 × 26.1 cm
National Archives of Canada, PA-165863

Graham Greene 21 May 1964
Gelatin silver print (emulsion-texture-enhanced)
32.8 × 24.3 cm
National Archives of Canada, PA-165814

Sydney Greenstreet 8 February 1946
Matte gelatin silver, printed later
42.8 × 35.1 cm
National Archives of Canada, PA-165873

Grey Owl (Archibald Belaney) 27 February 1937
Matte gelatin silver, printed 1989
50.0 × 40.2 cm
National Gallery of Canada
Gift of the artist

Jascha Heifetz 9 July 1957
Gelatin silver, printed later
49.7 × 39.3 cm
National Archives of Canada, PA-165937

Johan Helders 2 April 1938
Matte gelatin silver, printed later
50.4 × 40.4 cm
National Archives of Canada, PA-138574

158

Ernest Hemingway 15 March 1957
Gelatin silver (emulsion-texture-enhanced),
    printed later
27.2 × 21.6 cm
National Archives of Canada, PA-165815

George Hill 9 November 1945
Gelatin silver, printed later
49.5 × 39.6 cm
National Archives of Canada, PA-165936

Harold L. Ickes 15 March 1944
Gelatin silver print
32.3 × 26.0 cm
National Archives of Canada, PA-165857

Augustus John 18 July 1954
Gelatin silver, printed later
42.0 × 34.8 cm
National Archives of Canada, PA-165891

Edmond Joly de Lotbinière 20 July 1961
Gelatin silver print (emulsion-texture-enhanced)
20.2 × 15.3 cm
National Archives of Canada, PA-165874

Louis Jouvet 28 May 1949
Matte gelatin silver, printed 1988
50.1 × 40.2 cm
National Gallery of Canada
Gift of the artist

Karen Kain July–August 1977
Gelatin silver print
49.7 × 35.9 cm
National Archives of Canada, PA-165912

Boris Karloff 10 February 1946
Matte gelatin silver, printed 1988
49.1 × 40.2 cm
National Gallery of Canada
Gift of the artist

Estrellita Karsh 19 January 1970
Gelatin silver print (emulsion-texture-enhanced)
35.3 × 27.9 cm
National Archives of Canada, PA-165885

Estrellita Karsh 1963
Gelatin silver print (emulsion-texture-enhanced)
42.7 × 34.4 cm
National Archives of Canada, PA-165933

Yousuf Karsh (Self-portrait) 25 August 1976
Gelatin silver, printed 1989
27.1 × 21.6 cm
Collection of the artist

Helen Keller, with Polly Thomson 8 March 1948
Gelatin silver (emulsion-texture-enhanced),
    printed later
18.8 × 22.9 cm
National Archives of Canada, PA-165904

Edward Kennedy 16 February 1968
Gelatin silver print (emulsion-texture-enhanced)
20.2 × 20.4 cm
National Archives of Canada, PA-165871

William Lyon Mackenzie King, with Pat
    25 November 1940
Matte gelatin silver print
11.0 × 8.0 cm
National Archives of Canada, PA-165817

*Roppeita Kita, with grandson Nagayo
    Kita* November 1969
Matte gelatin silver, printed 1988
50.4 × 40.2 cm
National Gallery of Canada
Gift of the artist

Fritz Kreisler 29 November 1955
Gelatin silver print (emulsion-texture-enhanced)
25.1 × 20.4 cm
National Archives of Canada, PA-165920

Charles Laughton June 1958
Matte gelatin silver, printed later
50.5 × 40.4 cm
National Archives of Canada, PA-165818

Stephen Leacock 18 August 1941
Gelatin silver, printed later
50.3 × 39.7 cm
National Archives of Canada, PA-165935

The Lesson before 1940
Matte gelatin silver print
41.8 × 33.4 cm
Collection of the artist

John L. Lewis 4 May 1944
Gelatin silver print (emulsion-texture-enhanced)
24.1 × 19.3 cm
National Archives of Canada, PA-165819

Beatrice Lillie 18 March 1948
Gelatin silver print (emulsion-texture-enhanced)
33.3 × 26.5 cm
National Archives of Canada, PA-165928

Frederick Loewe 10 April 1959
Gelatin silver print (emulsion-texture-enhanced)
28.5 × 21.1 cm
National Archives of Canada, PA-165922

Peter Lorre 3 February 1946
Matte gelatin silver, printed 1988
44.5 × 40.2 cm
National Gallery of Canada
Gift of the artist

Harry H. Lunn, Jr. 10 August 1978
Gelatin silver print
35.4 × 28.0 cm
National Archives of Canada, PA-165820

Ludmilla Lvova (Betty Low) 16 August 1939
Gelatin silver print (emulsion-texture-enhanced)
39.4 × 32.6 cm
National Archives of Canada, PA-165925

Ernest MacMillan 8 February 1943
Gelatin silver print (emulsion-texture-enhanced)
32.9 × 26.1 cm
National Archives of Canada, PA-165861

Agnes MacPhail 15 May 1934
Gelatin silver print (emulsion-texture-enhanced)
23.9 × 19.1 cm
National Archives of Canada, PA-165870

Anna Magnani May 1958
Matte gelatin silver, printed 1988
50.2 × 39.5 cm
National Gallery of Canada
Gift of the artist

A.J. Major 27 August 1941
Gelatin silver print (emulsion-texture-enhanced)
23.9 × 19.1 cm
National Archives of Canada, PA-165891

André Malraux 3 June 1954
Gelatin silver, printed 1988
49.9 × 40.2 cm
National Gallery of Canada
Gift of the artist

Man Ray 29 March 1965
Matte gelatin silver, printed 1987
50.0 × 40.3 cm
National Gallery of Canada
Gift of the artist

Marcel Marceau 7 February 1956
Gelatin silver print
23.9 × 19.2 cm
National Archives of Canada, PA-165889

Mary Martin 21 March 1960
Matte gelatin silver, printed 1988
27.2 × 34.9 cm
National Gallery of Canada
Gift of the artist

W. Somerset Maugham 30 October 1950
Gelatin silver print (emulsion-texture-enhanced)
32.8 × 25.4 cm
National Archives of Canada, PA-165821

François Mauriac 1 April 1965
Matte gelatin silver, printed 1988
27.4 × 34.9 cm
National Gallery of Canada
Gift of the artist

Thomas McDonough 25 May 1955
Gelatin silver print (emulsion-texture-enhanced)
24.0 × 19.2 cm
National Archives of Canada, PA-165822

Gian Carlo Menotti 11 March 1956
Matte gelatin silver, printed 1988
46.4 × 35.0 cm
National Gallery of Canada
Gift of the artist

Ludwig Mies van der Rohe 1 July 1962
Gelatin silver print (emulsion-texture-enhanced)
32.8 × 26.1 cm
National Archives of Canada, PA-165916

Norman F. Miller 3 July 1962
Gelatin silver print (emulsion-texture-enhanced)
19.1 × 23.8 cm
National Archives of Canada, PA-165866

Joan Miró 30 March 1965
Gelatin silver (emulsion-texture-enhanced),
    printed later
27.8 × 21.7 cm
National Archives of Canada, PA-165902

*Muscular Dystrophy Association Poster Child:
    Rocco (Rocky) Arizzi* 1979
Gelatin silver print
50.5 × 40.6 cm
National Archives of Canada, PA-165939

*Muscular Dystrophy Association Poster Child:
    Rocco (Rocky) Arizzi and His Mother* 1979
Gelatin silver print
50.4 × 40.6 cm
National Archives of Canada, PA-165914

*Muscular Dystrophy Association Poster Child:
    Rocco (Rocky) Arizzi and His Mother* 1979
Gelatin silver print
50.6 × 40.6 cm
National Archives of Canada, PA-165940

*Muscular Dystrophy Association Summer Camp,
    N.Y.* 1979
Gelatin silver print
40.6 × 50.5 cm
National Archives of Canada, PA-165832

*Muscular Dystrophy Clinic, Lenox Hill Hospital,
    New York* 1979
Gelatin silver print
40.6 × 50.5 cm
National Archives of Canada, PA-165941

*Muscular Dystrophy Clinic, Lenox Hill Hospital,
    New York* 1979
Gelatin silver print
40.7 × 50.4 cm
National Archives of Canada, PA-165830

Muscular Dystrophy Clinic, Lenox Hill Hospital,
   New York: Learning the Diagnosis 1979
Gelatin silver print
40.6 × 50.4 cm
National Archives of Canada, PA-165907

Muscular Dystrophy Clinic, Lenox Hill Hospital,
   New York: Learning the Diagnosis 1979
Gelatin silver print
40.6 × 50.4 cm
National Archives of Canada, PA-165905

Muscular Dystrophy Clinic, Lenox Hill Hospital,
   New York: Learning the Diagnosis 1979
Gelatin silver print
40.6 × 50.4 cm
National Archives of Canada, PA-165906

Muscular Dystrophy Clinic, Lenox Hill Hospital,
   New York: Learning the Diagnosis 1979
Gelatin silver print
40.6 × 50.4 cm
National Archives of Canada, PA-165942

Myself When Young before September 1936
Matte gelatin silver print
41.5 × 33.6 cm
Collection of the artist

Vladimir Nabokov 3 November 1972
Gelatin silver, printed 1988
50.3 × 39.9 cm
National Gallery of Canada
Gift of the artist

Patricia Neal 4 December 1985
Gelatin silver print
40.6 × 50.4 cm
National Archives of Canada, PA-165908

Margaret O'Brien 24 February 1946
Gelatin silver print (emulsion-texture-enhanced)
50.4 × 37.6 cm
National Archives of Canada, PA-165934

Georgia O'Keeffe 18 March 1956
Gelatin silver (emulsion-texture-enhanced),
   printed later
27.7 × 21.6 cm
National Archives of Canada, PA-165823

Robert Oppenheimer 9 February 1956
Matte gelatin silver, printed 1988
35.1 × 27.3 cm
National Gallery of Canada
Gift of the artist

Ottawa Little Theatre: "The Bear" 26 April 1935
Gelatin silver, printed later
25.4 × 32.1 cm
National Archives of Canada, PA-165894

Ottawa Little Theatre: "Romeo and Juliet"
   24 November 1933
Gelatin silver, printed later
23.9 × 27.0 cm
National Archives of Canada, PA-165877

Ottawa Little Theatre: "Les Sœurs Guedonec"
   22 April 1936
Gelatin silver, printed later
24.1 × 31.8 cm
National Archives of Canada, PA-165836

Ottawa Little Theatre: "Saint Joan"
   18 November 1936
Gelatin silver print (emulsion-texture-enhanced)
30.4 × 22.9 cm
National Archives of Canada, PA-165843

Ottawa Little Theatre: "Street Scene"
    19 January 1937
Gelatin silver, printed later
24.4 × 30.3 cm
National Archives of Canada, PA-165893

Lester B. Pearson 23 November 1957
Matte gelatin silver, printed 1988
49.6 × 40.2 cm
National Gallery of Canada
Gift of the artist

Gregory Peck 31 January 1946
Gelatin silver print (emulsion-texture-enhanced)
35.4 × 28.1 cm
National Archives of Canada, PA-165886

Maiya Mikhailovna Plisetskaya
    March–April 1963
Gelatin silver print
35.3 × 27.8 cm
National Archives of Canada, PA-165876

Georges Pompidou 21 September 1965
Matte gelatin silver, printed 1988
50.1 × 40.2 cm
National Gallery of Canada
Gift of the artist

J.B. Priestley 12 July 1949
Gelatin silver, printed later
39.2 × 43.6 cm
National Archives of Canada, PA-165932

Emilio Pucci 9 July 1967
Gelatin silver print (emulsion-texture-enhanced)
24.0 × 19.1 cm
National Archives of Canada, PA-165824

Louis Quarles 6 May 1965
Gelatin silver print (emulsion-texture-enhanced)
22.6 × 19.1 cm
National Archives of Canada, PA-165825

Prince Rainier III and Princess Grace of
    Monaco 22 September 1956
Gelatin silver print (emulsion-texture-enhanced)
34.6 × 34.7 cm
National Archives of Canada, PA-165872

Henry Rand 14 September 1960
Gelatin silver print (emulsion-texture-enhanced)
32.9 × 26.2 cm
National Archives of Canada, PA-165882

Edgar Ritchie, Gordon Robertson, Arnold Smith,
    and Jules Léger, The Rideau Club, Ottawa
    3 August 1973
Gelatin silver print
23.7 × 19.1 cm
National Archives of Canada, PA-165869

Jerome Robbins 21 October 1986
Gelatin silver print
27.9 × 21.6 cm
National Archives of Canada, PA-165868

Winthrop Rockefeller, Winston Churchill, and a
    Trustee of the Williamsburg Foundation
    7 December 1955
Gelatin silver print
26.0 × 33.1 cm
National Archives of Canada, PA-165807

Norman Rockwell 12 February 1956
Gelatin silver, printed 1988
31.3 × 25.3 cm
National Gallery of Canada
Gift of the artist

Richard Rodgers and Oscar Hammerstein
   10 February 1950
Gelatin silver, printed later
49.2 × 39.3 cm
National Archives of Canada, PA-165931

James Rorimer September 1964
Gelatin silver print (emulsion-texture-enhanced)
32.8 × 26.1 cm
National Archives of Canada, PA-165859

Mstislav Rostropovitch October 1974
Gelatin silver print
32.8 × 26.2 cm
National Archives of Canada, PA-165826

Artur Rubinstein's Hands 31 October 1945
Matte gelatin silver, printed 1989
31.6 × 24.8 cm
Collection of the artist

Bertrand Russell 13 July 1949
Gelatin silver, printed later
33.6 × 40.8 cm
National Archives of Canada, PA-165827

Andrei Sakharov 13 February 1989
Matte gelatin silver print
28.0 × 21.6 cm
Collection of the artist

Andrei Sakharov and Yelena Bonner
   13 February 1989
Matte gelatin silver print
28.0 × 21.7 cm
Collection of the artist

Pierre Salinger 24 January 1962
Gelatin silver print (emulsion-texture-enhanced)
24.0 × 19.1 cm
National Archives of Canada, PA-165860

B.K. Sandwell 22 Mar 1939
Gelatin silver, printed later
37.8 × 32.9 cm
National Archives of Canada, PA-165840

Joseph Schaffner 17 June 1970
Gelatin silver print (emulsion-texture-enhanced)
19.0 × 22.2 cm
National Archives of Canada, PA-165841

Albert Schweitzer 19 June 1954
Matte gelatin silver, printed 1988
49.7 × 40.1 cm
National Gallery of Canada
Gift of the artist

Barbara Ann Scott 26 November 1946
Gelatin silver print
32.3 × 25.9 cm
National Archives of Canada, PA-165917

Barbara Ann Scott 26 November 1946
Gelatin silver print (emulsion-texture-enhanced)
23.8 × 18.3 cm
National Archives of Canada, PA-165921

Duncan Campbell Scott 16 September 1933
Gelatin silver, printed later
26.5 × 32.1 cm
National Archives of Canada, PA-165842

George Bernard Shaw 12 September–12
   November 1943
Gelatin silver (emulsion-texture-enhanced),
   printed later
27.8 × 21.6 cm
National Archives of Canada, PA-165903

Jean Sibelius 30 July 1949
Matte gelatin silver, printed 1988
49.8 × 40.1 cm
National Gallery of Canada
Gift of the artist

Vilhjalmur Stefansson 14 May 1947
Gelatin silver print (emulsion-texture-enhanced)
32.8 × 26.1 cm
National Archives of Canada, PA-165878

Igor Stravinsky 20 March 1956
Gelatin silver print (emulsion-texture-enhanced)
25.5 × 20.3 cm
National Archives of Canada, PA-165865

Lenore Tawney 14 November 1959
Matte gelatin silver, printed 1988
27.2 × 34.6 cm
National Gallery of Canada
Gift of the artist

Francis Henry Taylor 20 June 1957
Matte gelatin silver, printed 1988
49.7 × 40.1 cm
National Gallery of Canada
Gift of the artist

Shin'ichirō Tomonaga November 1969
Matte gelatin silver, printed 1988
39.5 × 48.4 cm
National Gallery of Canada
Gift of the artist

Pierre Elliott Trudeau 4 November 1968
Gelatin silver, printed 1988
31.5 × 25.1 cm
National Gallery of Canada
Gift of the artist

Desmond Tutu 20 December 1984
Matte gelatin silver print
50.3 × 40.4 cm
National Archives of Canada, PA-165911

Peter Ustinov 22 October 1971
Matte gelatin silver print
50.5 × 40.5 cm
National Archives of Canada, PA-165856

Maria Helena Vieira da Silva 23 September 1965
Gelatin silver print (emulsion-texture-enhanced)
25.8 × 20.4 cm
National Archives of Canada, PA-165828

Roman Vishniac 22 February 1971
Matte gelatin silver, printed 1988
50.1 × 39.5 cm
National Gallery of Canada
Gift of the artist

John Walker 3 November 1964
Gelatin silver print (emulsion-texture-enhanced)
32.8 × 25.5 cm
National Archives of Canada, PA-165918

Andy Warhol 21 November 1979
Gelatin silver print (emulsion-texture-enhanced)
50.0 × 39.9 cm
National Archives of Canada, PA-165930

Bradford Washburn 6 February 1966
Gelatin silver print (emulsion-texture-enhanced)
24.0 × 19.1 cm
National Archives of Canada, PA-165887

Thomas J. Watson 28 January 1948
Gelatin silver print (emulsion-texture-enhanced)
30.1 × 22.9 cm
National Archives of Canada, PA-165927

Evelyn Waugh 8 July 1964
Matte gelatin silver, printed 1988
40.1 × 49.8 cm
National Gallery of Canada
Gift of the artist

H.G. Wells 12 September–12 November 1943
Gelatin silver, printed later
31.8 × 25.9 cm
National Archives of Canada, PA-165929

Thornton Wilder 24 May 1956
Gelatin silver, printed later
49.7 × 39.1 cm
National Archives of Canada, PA-165848

The Duchess of Windsor 8 June 1971
Matte gelatin silver, printed 1988
35.1 × 27.3 cm
National Gallery of Canada
Gift of the artist

Marguerite Yourcenar 19 September 1987
Matte gelatin silver print
50.1 × 40.2 cm
Collection of the artist

Ossip Zadkine 4 April 1965
Matte gelatin silver, printed 1987
27.9 × 21.5 cm
National Gallery of Canada
Gift of the artist

"Zulu": Drummers June–July 1963
Gelatin silver, printed 1989
40.3 × 39.9 cm
Collection of the artist

"Zulu": Extra June–July 1963
Gelatin silver, printed 1989
40.0 × 39.3 cm
Collection of the artist

"Zulu": Extra June–July 1963
Gelatin silver, printed 1989
40.5 × 38.2 cm
Collection of the artist

"Zulu": Ulla Jacobsson, with Extras
   June–July 1963
Gelatin silver, printed 1989
40.8 × 39.8 cm
Collection of the artist

166

Biographical Notes

Prepared by David Strong

Frontispiece
Winston Churchill 1941
British statesman, orator and historian (1874–1965). Served in the Boer War and World War I, and led Britain as Prime Minister through World War II and from 1951–55. Author of *A History of the English Speaking Peoples*.

Plate 1
Johan Helders 1938
Dutch-born Canadian hotel caterer and photographer (1888–1956). Arrived in Canada in 1924. Maître d'hôtel, Château Laurier, Ottawa, 1926–39. One of Canada's finest pictorialist photographers during the late 1920s and early 1930s.

Plate 2
Ruth Draper 1936
American actress (1884–1956). Achieved fame as a solo performer of her own dramatic monologues. After her New York debut in 1917, she toured the world continuously for nearly forty years.

Plate 3
Bertrand Russell 1949
British mathematician, philosopher and social activist (1872–1970). Books include *Principia Mathematica* (with Alfred North Whitehead) and *History of Western Philosophy*. Imprisoned twice: for his pacifism, and for anti-nuclear civil disobedience.

Plate 4
William Lyon Mackenzie King, with Pat 1940
Canadian politician and statesman (1874–1950). Prime Minister of Canada, 1921–30, 1935–48. Leader of the Liberal Party from 1919. Introduced unemployment insurance, 1940.

Plate 5
Lysle Courtenay 1933
Canadian interior decorator (1898–1971). A set designer for the Ottawa Little Theatre during the 1930s.

Plate 6
John Buchan 1938
British author and statesman Lord Tweedsmuir (1875–1940). Known for adventure stories, notably *Thirty-Nine Steps*. Canadian Governor General, 1935–40. Inaugurated Governor General's literary award.

Plate 7
Grey Owl (Archibald Belaney) 1937
English-born writer and conservationist (1888–1938). Moved to Canada at age seventeen. Adopted the name Grey Owl and the background of a half-Apache. Lived with the Ojibways, worked in the national parks, and wrote books including *Pilgrims of the Wild*.

Plate 8
John L. Lewis 1944
American labour leader (1880–1969). Miner from age fifteen. President of United Mine Workers of America, founder of the Congress of Industrial Organizations (CIO). Awarded Presidential Medal of Freedom, 1964.

Plate 9
Ansel Adams 1977
American photographer (1902–84). Known for technically brilliant images of the American landscape. Developed the Zone System, and the idea of pre-visualization. Co-founder, Group f/64, 1932; and of the Department of Photography, Museum of Modern Art, New York, 1940.

Plate 10
Jean Sibelius 1949
Finnish composer (1865–1957). A major figure in the development of the symphony, and a strong nationalist. Known for such works as *Finlandia* and *Tapiola*. Provided with a life pension by the Finnish government from age thirty-two.

Plate 11
Christian Dior 1954
French couturier (1905–57). Behind the post-war rise to dominance of the French fashion industry, beginning with the "New Look" (lowered hemlines, small shoulders, natural waistline) of 1947.

Plate 12
Charles Laughton 1958
British-born actor (1899–1962). Known for roles in such films as *Mutiny on the Bounty* (Best Actor, New York Film Critics) and *Witness for the Prosecution*. Became a U.S. citizen in 1950.

Plate 13
Jean-Louis Barrault 1949
French actor, stage producer and director (b. 1910). Directed the Odéon, which became the Théâtre de France. His outstanding film role was the mime in *Les Enfants du Paradis*.

Plate 14
Gian Carlo Menotti 1956
Italian-born composer (b. 1911). Known for popular operas and chamber music. Guggenheim awards 1946, 1947; Pulitzer prizes for *The Consul* and *The Saint of Bleeker Street*. Moved to the United States in 1928.

Plate 15
Anna Magnani 1958
Italian film actress (1908–73). Famous for portrayals of earthy, working-class women. Starred in films including Roberto Rossellini's *Open City* (*Roma città aperta*) and *Rose Tattoo* (Academy award, Best Actress).

Plate 16
Katharine Cornell 1947
American stage actress-manager (1893–1974). Co-founder, Cornell and McClintic Productions. Her most famous role was Elizabeth Barrett in *The Barretts of Wimpole Street*.

Plate 17
Jacob Epstein 1955
American-born sculptor (1880–1959). Moved to Britain, 1905; founding member of the London Group. Known for massive stone carvings, and smaller bronzes of famous personages, for example, Albert Einstein.

Plate 18
Peter Lorre 1946
Hungarian-born American film actor (1904–64).
His soft, menacing voice brought a series of
sinister characters to life, beginning with a
psychotic child murderer in Fritz Lang's *M*. Best
known for roles opposite Humphrey Bogart in *The
Maltese Falcon* and *Casablanca*.

Plate 19
Robert Oppenheimer 1956
American physicist (1904–67). Director of Los
Alamos laboratory where the first atomic bomb
was developed. Director, Institute for Advanced
Study, Princeton. Author of *The Open Mind* and
Science and the Common Understanding.

Plate 20
Camillien Houde 1952
Canadian politician (1889–1958). Mayor of Montreal, known as "Monsieur Montréal." Interned by
the federal government, 1940–44, for his opposition to registration for military service. On his
release, a crowd of 100,000 welcomed him.
Photographed for the *Maclean's* series, "Face of
Canada."

Plate 21
Georges Pompidou 1965
French statesman and politician (1911–74). Prime
Minister of France, 1962–68; President, 1969–
74. Assisted Charles de Gaulle in drafting the
constitution of France's Fifth Republic.

Plate 22
Graham Greene 1964
British writer and diplomat (b. 1904). Worked for
the Foreign Office during World War II; member
of the Panamanian delegation, 1977. Novels
include *The Power and the Glory* and *The Third
Man*.

Plate 23
Charles de Gaulle 1944
French statesman and military general (1890–
1970). President of France, 1958–69. In exile
during World War II, he led the Free French from
London. Architect of France's Fifth Republic.

Plate 24
*Winthrop Rockefeller, Winston Churchill, and a
Trustee of the Williamsburg Foundation* 1955
On the occasion of Churchill's acceptance of the
Williamsburg (Virginia) Foundation award at
Draper's Hall, London.

Plate 25
Ernest Hemingway 1957
American writer (1899–1961). Newspaper corres-
pondent during the Spanish Civil War and World
War II. Novels include *For Whom the Bell Tolls*
and *The Old Man and the Sea* (Pulitzer prize).
Awarded Nobel prize for literature, 1954.

Plate 26
J. Paul Getty 1964
American business executive and art collector
(1892–1976). President and principal owner,
Getty Oil Company. Founder and trustee, J. Paul
Getty Museum.

Plate 27
W. Somerset Maugham 1950
English writer (1874–1965). Known for such
novels as *Of Human Bondage*, *The Moon and
Sixpence*, and *The Razor's Edge*. Autobiographical
works include *A Writer's Notebook*.

Plate 28
Louis Jouvet 1949
French stage actor, director, set and lighting
designer (1887–1951). Became director of the
Comédie des Champs-Élysées in 1924. One of the
most respected figures in twentieth century
French theatre.

Plate 29
Mstislav Rostropovitch 1974
Russian-born cellist and conductor (b. 1927).
Recipient of four Grammy awards, and a Knight
Commander of the Order of the British Empire.
Conductor, National Symphony Orchestra,
Washington, D.C.

Plate 30
Clark Gable 1948
American actor (1901–60). Famous for roles as a
romantic rogue in such films as *It Happened One
Night* (Academy award, Best Actor) and, most
memorably, as Rhett Butler in *Gone with the
Wind*.

Plate 31
Peter Ustinov 1971
English actor, director, playwright, screenwriter
and novelist (b. 1921). Work includes *Romanoff
and Juliet* (British Critics' Best Play award),
Spartacus (Academy award, Best Supporting
Actor), and *Peter and the Wolf* (Grammy award).

Plate 32
Elizabeth Arden 1948
Canadian-born entrepreneur (1878?–1966).
Moved to New York City, 1908. The "High
Priestess of Beauty" created a cosmetics empire
by pioneering innovative marketing and adverti-
sing techniques.

Plate 33
Josef Albers 1966
German painter, poet, and art theoretician (1888–
1976). Innovator in Colour Field painting and Op
art. Teacher at the Bauhaus. In the 1930s moved
to the United States, and taught at Black Mountain
College.

Plate 34
Man Ray 1965
American photographer, filmmaker and painter
(1890–1976). Associated with the Dadaists and
Surrealists. A ceaseless experimenter, known
especially for his solarized photographs and
Rayographs.

Plate 35
Ossip Zadkine 1965
Russian-born sculptor (1890–1967). Member of
the Paris School. Lived in the United States during
World War II, teaching at the Art Students League,
New York. Sculpture prize, 1950 Venice Biennale.

Plate 36
Pablo Casals 1954
Spanish cellist, composer and conductor (1876–
1973). Famous for interpretations of J.S. Bach.
Formed an internationally renowned trio with
pianist Alfred Cortot and violinist Jacques
Thibaud.

Plate 37
Georgia O'Keeffe 1956
American artist (1887–1986). Known for boldy
coloured paintings of natural forms. Work first
exhibited by Alfred Stieglitz, 1916. Major retrospective, Whitney Museum of American Art, 1970.

Plate 38
Garrison Club, Quebec City 1953
Photographed for the *Maclean's* series "Face of
Canada."

Plate 39
Maria Helena Vieira da Silva 1965
Portuguese-born painter (b. 1908). Known for
abstractions of architecture and space. Emigrated
to France, 1928. Grand prix national des Arts,
Paris, and elected Chevalier of the Légion
d'honneur.

Plate 40
Konrad Adenauer 1964
German politician and statesman (1876–1967).
First chancellor of the Federal Republic of Germany. Twice imprisoned by the Nazis. Presided over Germany's post-war reconstruction and reconciliation with European neighbours.

Plate 41
Robertson Davies 1977
Canadian novelist and journalist (b. 1913). Publisher of the Peterborough *Examiner*. Professor, University of Toronto. Novels include *Leaven of Malice* (Stephen Leacock medal for humour) and *The Manticore* (Governor General's award).

Plate 42
Cecil B. deMille 1956
American film producer-director (1881–1959). Famous for spectacular productions on epic themes, such as *The Ten Commandments* and *The Greatest Show on Earth* (Academy award, Best Picture).

Plate 43
Georges Enesco 1954
Romanian violinist and composer (1881–1955). Known for interpretations of J.S. Bach, and for compositions inspired by Romanian folk music. Principal teacher of the violinist Yehudi Menuhin.

Plate 44
Atlas Steels, Welland, Ontario: Kenneth (Tiny) Stirtzinger 1950
Photographed as part of an assignment for Atlas Steels.

Plate 45
Ford Canada, Windsor: Paint Shop 1951
From a publicity series commissioned by Ford.

Plate 46
Muscular Dystrophy Clinic, Lenox Hill Hospital, New York 1979
Part of a series made for the Muscular Dystrophy Association.

Plate 47
Muscular Dystrophy Association Summer Camp, N.Y. 1979
Part of a series made for the Muscular Dystrophy Association.

Plate 48
Leon Charash 1980
American pediatric neurologist (b. 1927). Active in the fight against muscular dystrophy.

Plate 49
The Duchess of Windsor 1971
American divorcée, formerly Mrs. Wallis Warfield Spencer Simpson (1896–1986). The King of England, Edward VIII, abdicated the throne in 1936 in order to marry her.

Plate 50
Emilio Pucci 1967
Italian fashion designer and politician (b. 1914). Noted for sportswear collections. Recipient, *Harper's Bazaar* medallion and the Nieman Marcus award. Member, Italian parliament; city counsellor, Florence.

Plate 51
Louis Quarles 1965
American lawyer and yachtsman (1883–1972). Specialized in patent law.

Plate 52

Kenneth M. Brinkhous, Robert D. Langdell, and Robert H. Wagner 1978

American pathologists, specializing in blood disorders, University of North Carolina. Kenneth M. Brinkhous (b. 1908) – International Heart Research award, 1969. Robert D. Langdell (b. 1924) – editor, *Transfusion*, 1972–82. Robert H. Wagner (b. 1921) – International Prize, French Association of Hæmophilia, 1977.

Plate 53

Harry H. Lunn, Jr. 1978

American art dealer (b. 1933). Specializing in photography, and nineteenth and twentieth century prints and drawings.

Plate 54

Marguerite Yourcenar 1987

French novelist and essayist (1903–87). Known for novels such as *Coup de Grace* and *Memoirs of Hadrian* (prix Fémina). Translator of Greek, and of Virginia Woolf and Henry James. First woman elected to the Académie française, 1980.

Plage 55

Gérard Depardieu 1985

French stage, television and film actor (b. 1948). Known for roles in films such as *Police* (Best Actor, Venice Film Festival), and *Under the Sun of Satan* (Palme d'or, Cannes).

Plate 56

Thomas McDonough 1955

Canadian clergyman (b. 1924). Dominican father. Served in Ottawa and Port Credit, Ontario.

List of Illustrations

Acknowledgements

James Borcoman

This exhibition began life as the Karsh gift, a group of photographs generously donated by Yousuf Karsh to the National Gallery of Canada in 1989. Thanks to the encouragement of Richard Huyda, Director General of Public Programs at the National Archives, whose long-term commitment to Karsh's work first fueled the idea of a collaboration between the Archives and the Gallery, the exhibition has been expanded into a full-scale retrospective. As a result, National Archives has kindly made its Karsh Collection available for extensive loans to the exhibition, in addition to sharing the cost of the project. A special thanks is therefore due to the staff of the National Archives's Documentary Art and Photography department: Lilly Koltun, Marie-France Fortier, Brian Carey, Andrew Rodger, Guy Tessier, Ed Thompkins, Joy Houston, Ginette Bonneau, Linda Cassidy, Lynne Rioux, Elizabeth Krug, and Mae Borris.

We are grateful to Yousuf Karsh for also lending works from his private collection for the retrospective, and for the advice, time, and care that he, along with his wife, Estrellita, his assistant, Jerry Fielder, and his secretary, Mary Alderman, have taken in assisting in its organization.

At the National Gallery, thanks are due to the dedication of the staff of the Photographs Collection: Barbara Boutin, Division Secretary, Hazel Mackenzie, Documentation Officer, David Strong, Curatorial Assistant, John McElhone, Photographic Conservator, and Michael Gribbon, Collections Coordinator of Prints, Drawings, and Photographs. In the Exhibitions Division, we are grateful to Catherine Sage and Jacques Naud for the coordination of the exhibition. The creative talents of the Exhibition Design team of the Gallery, including Tom Thurston, Allan Todd, Tina Gimenez, and Tracy Pritchard also deserve acknowledgement.

A book such as this can be achieved only with the help of dedicated and talented people. In this respect, the contributions of Serge Thériault, Head of Publications at the National Gallery, who also brought a patient guidance to the project, and of editors Susan McMaster, Hélène Papineau, and Claire Rochon, Photograph Editor Colleen Evans, and Production Manager Jean-Guy Bergeron are deeply appreciated. Eiko Emori deserves our gratitude for her elegant and intelligent design. Finally, Bryan Goudie and John Rumbolt must be given special mention for the painstaking care they have taken over the separations and plates for the book.

Canadian Cataloguing in Publication Data

Borcoman, James.
Karsh, the art of the portrait.

Issued also in French under title: Karsh, l'art du portrait.

ISBN 0-88884-591-X (bound)—0-88884-600-2 (pbk.)

1. Karsh, Yousuf, 1908-   –Exhibitions. 2. Photography–
Portraits–Exhibitions. 3. Photography, Artistic–Exhibitions.
I. National Gallery of Canada. II. Title.

TR680 .B67 1989   779'.2'0924   CIP 89-099500-1

Published in conjunction with the exhibition *Karsh: The Art of the Portrait*, organized by the National Gallery of Canada in collaboration with the National Archives of Canada, and presented in Ottawa from 29 June to 4 September 1989.

© National Gallery of Canada for the Corporation of National Museums of Canada, Ottawa, 1989.

Design: Eiko Emori
Film: Running and Ojala
Printing: M.O.M. Printing

Available from your local bookseller or
The Bookstore
National Gallery of Canada
380 Sussex Drive, Box 427, Station A
Ottawa K1N 9N4

PRINTED IN CANADA

Cover: *Grey Owl (Archibald Belaney)* 1937
Frontispiece: *Winston Churchill* 1941
Back cover: *Yousuf Karsh (Self-portrait)* 1976